How to Succeed on the Michigan Test Battery

Test Taker's Checklist

Read directions carefully. Don't start out with a false assumption. Time is included to allow you to read the directions. Be sure you understand what is being asked.

Consider all choices. You must choose the *best* choice, not just a good choice.

Avoid superstitions. There is no pattern on a standardized test like the Michigan Test. If you have just answered B four times in a row, the next answer has the same chance of being A, B, C, or D. Don't make choices for a problem based on answers from other problems.

Mark your answer sheet clearly. Use a soft lead pencil (No. 2) and blacken the choice completely. If you must erase an answer, erase it completely.

Guess if you don't know the answer. Since no points are deducted for guessing, be sure you have marked your answer sheet completely.

Concentrate. Don't talk. Concentrate your attention. Don't look at anything in the test room except your test materials. Don't think about your score or your future. If you do, force your mind to return to the problem you are working on.

Budget your time. Calculate the time you may spend on each question so that you have enough time to complete all of the questions on the test. Don't spend too much time on a question you can't answer.

Don't cheat. In spite of opportunity, knowledge that others are cheating, desire to help a friend, or fear that you will not make a good score, don't cheat. In the United States it is considered very serious. If you are discovered, your test materials will be taken, you will not be allowed to finish the examination, and your answer sheet will not be scored.

Think positively. Your attitude will influence your success on the Michigan Test. Remember, you are not trying to score 100 percent. No one knows everything. If you have studied the material in this book and other books, you should feel prepared. Do your best!

HOW TO PREPARE FOR THE
MICHIGAN
TEST BATTERY

**Covers all 3 tests in the Michigan Test Battery:
Aural Comprehension • English Proficiency • Composition**

By Pamela J. Sharpe

Founding Director
The American Language Institute
University of Toledo

Barron's Educational Series, Inc.

To all of the students at the American Language Institute who asked that this book be written.

All inquiries should be addressed to:
Barron's Educational Series, Inc.
250 Wireless Boulevard
Hauppauge, New York 11788

Library of Congress Catalog Card No. 81-22816

ISBN-13: 978-0-8120-2419-7
ISBN-10: 0-8120-2419-2

Library of Congress Cataloging-in-Publication Data
Sharpe, Pamela J.

   Barron's How to prepare for the Michigan test battery.
      1. English language—Text-books for foreigners.
   2. English language—Examinations.   I. Title.   II. Title:
How to prepare for the Michigan test battery.
III. Title: Michigan test battery.
PE1128.S49   428'.007'6   81-22816
ISBN 0-8120-2419-2   AACR2

PRINTED IN THE UNITED STATES OF AMERICA
19 18 17 16

Contents

Acknowledgments

Grateful acknowledgment is made to the following publishers and authors for permission to adapt copyrighted materials:

Doubleday and Company, Inc., for excerpts adapted from "What about the Midnight Ride of William Dawes," "The Continuing Search for the Santa Maria," "Teacher Expectations and Student Learning," and "Wild Bill Hickok, Legendary Western Lawman," in *The People's Almanac* by David Wallace. Copyright © 1975 by David Wallace and Irving Wallace. Reprinted by permission of Doubleday and Company, Inc.

McGraw-Hill Book Company for excerpts adapted from "Sequoyah," in *Word People* by Nancy Caldwell Sorel. Copyright © 1970 by Nancy Caldwell Sorel. Reprinted by permission of McGraw-Hill Book Company.

Introduction

TO THE TEACHER

One of the most frustrating problems that we face as teachers of English as a second language (ESL) is that of demonstrating to our students the relationship between standardized tests like the Michigan Test Battery and the materials and activities we use in our classes. Too often, even good students judge the usefulness of a class merely by the number of familiar vocabulary words that appear on a standardized test.

This book is an effort to enlighten and encourage, as well as to provide practice. *Barron's How To Prepare for the Michigan Test Battery* can be used as a basic text for a language review course, as a supplementary text for listening, grammar, reading, and composition classes, or as a recommended text for self-study.

The section in this Introduction titled "Some Advice from the Author" was included to help students make informed decisions for themselves as they prepare to take the Michigan Test Battery. You may want to use it for a discussion class. Chapters Three, Five, and Seven titled "Continued Study. . ." were included to demonstrate the important relationship between classroom activities and the test.

TO THE STUDENT

The Michigan Test Battery is very important to you. It is used by many colleges and universities in the United States as a requirement for placement and admissions.

Many international students do not pass the Michigan Test Battery because they are not prepared when they take it. Some take it too soon. They have not studied enough English. Others have studied enough English, but have not studied for the test.

This book will not help you pass the Michigan Test Battery if you need to study more English. But if you have studied enough English, you are ready to prepare for the test.

This book will help you in three ways. It will help you

1. *to understand the Michigan Test Battery.* You will learn to understand the test directions and the types of questions found on the tests.

2. *to practice for the Michigan Test Battery.* You will take three model tests each for the Michigan Test of Aural Comprehension, the Michigan Test of English Language Proficiency, and the Michigan Composition Test.

3. *to learn how to study for the Michigan Test Battery*. You will be given many suggestions for continued study. Some of the suggestions will show you how to use your other English books to prepare for the Michigan Test Battery; other suggestions will show you how to use the homework from your English classes and your recreational activities to study.

SOME ADVICE FROM THE AUTHOR

As director of the American Language Institute of the University of Toledo, I gave advice to many international students. In this book, I would like to give you some advice on preparing for the Michigan Test Battery.

First, make a realistic decision. This means to make a decision based upon the facts. You should take the Michigan Test Battery when you have the best possible opportunity to make a high score. If you have studied English for only a few weeks, you should probably wait to take the test until you have studied more English. Although you may have been in the United States for a long time, if you have not been attending your English classes regularly, you should probably wait to take the test until you have reviewed your English. Can you read English well? Can you write it well? You will need these skills to succeed on the Michigan Test Battery and to succeed in a college or university in the United States.

If you are not sure whether you are ready to take the Michigan Test Battery, talk to a teacher you know well. Ask him or her to tell you the truth about your English so that you can decide whether to take the Michigan Test Battery now. Remember that it takes a long time to learn a language well. Try to be kind, patient, truthful, and realistic with yourself.

Don't try to share answers in the test room. Sharing answers during a test is called "cheating." In some countries, it is not considered serious. In the United States, it is very serious. If the examiner sees you, you and your friends may not be able to finish your tests. Worse still, you may not be able to apply for admission at the school where you cheated.

Think about this, too: if you pass your test by cheating, what will you do when you are admitted to a college or university? If the professor sees you cheating on a test in a college or university class, you and your friends may have to leave the school.

Use this book wisely. Don't try to memorize the questions in this book. The questions on the test that you take will be very similar to the questions in this book, but they will not be the same. What you should try to do is learn how to apply your knowledge to the test. Don't hurry through the model tests. While you are checking your answers with the answer key, think about them. Are you making repeated mistakes on the same kinds of questions? Why is the correct answer correct? If you can, study a little bit every day for several months. This will help you much more than studying a lot for only a few days.

Always use the answer sheets and complete each model test within the time suggested so that you can become accustomed to the test situation.

Remember that this book will help you most when you also follow the Suggestions for Continued Study given for each test.

Don't depend on good luck. I hope that you will have good luck on the Michigan Test Battery. But you should not depend on good luck alone. You should depend on yourself. You are the person who decides how to spend your time. If you decide to spend your time studying, you should be more confident when you take the Michigan Test Battery. You will bring good luck with you to the test because you will have prepared for it.

Pamela J. Sharpe

How to Use This Book

It is very easy to use this book.

1. Read Chapter One, "Questions and Answers Concerning the Michigan Test Battery."

2. Take Model Test One.
    The Michigan Test of Aural Comprehension: Chapter Two, pages 25-30.
    The Michigan Test of English Language Proficiency: Chapter Four, pages 69-87.
    The Michigan Composition Test: Chapter Six, page 166.

3. Check the Answer Keys and study the Explanatory Answers for each test.

4. Take Model Test Two.
    The Michigan Test of Aural Comprehension: Chapter Two, pages 25-30.
    The Michigan Test of English Language Proficiency: Chapter Four, pages 89-103.
    The Michigan Composition Test: Chapter Six, page 166.

5. Check the Answer Keys and study the Explanatory Answers for each test.

6. Take Model Test Three.
    The Michigan Test of Aural Comprehension: Chapter Two, pages 25-30.
    The Michigan Test of English Language Proficiency: Chapter Four, pages 105-118.
    The Michigan Composition Test: Chapter Six, page 167.

7. Check the Answer Keys and study the Explanatory Answers for each test.

8. Follow the Suggestions for Continued Study at the end of Chapters Three, Five, and Seven. You may also do the Optional Assignments.

Timetable for the Michigan Test Battery *

Total time: 130 minutes

Test One (25 minutes)	The Michigan Test of Aural Comprehension	90 questions
Test Two (75 minutes)	The Michigan Test of English Language Proficiency (MTELP)	100 questions
Test Three (30 minutes)	The Michigan Composition Test	1 page

*Note: Actual times will vary in accordance with the time the examiner needs to complete the preliminary work and begin the actual test. Format and timing subject to change.

Questions and Answers Concerning the Michigan Test Battery

CHAPTER 1

Questions and Answers Concerning the Michigan Test Battery

The following questions are commonly asked by international students as they prepare for the Michigan Test Battery. To help you, they have been answered here.

What Is a Test Battery?

A test battery is an examination that includes more than one test. For example, the Michigan Test Battery usually includes three tests:

> The Michigan Test of Aural Comprehension
> The Michigan Test of English Language Proficiency
> The Michigan Composition Test

What Is the Purpose of the Michigan Test Battery?

The Michigan Test Battery is a *standardized* test. *Standardized* means that it can be used by many colleges and universities throughout the United States and in other countries.

It is used to test proficiency, to assist in placement, and to measure progress. If it is used to test proficiency, your score helps your advisor or the admissions officer decide whether you know enough English to attend the university or whether you need additional English classes. If it is used to assist in placement, your score helps your advisor or teacher choose the best classes for you to attend. If it is used to measure progress, your score helps your English teacher and you know how much you have learned since your last test. It also helps your teacher plan the best lessons for your next class.

Which Language Skills Are Tested on the Michigan Test Battery?

The following language skills are tested on the Michigan Test Battery:
On the Michigan Test of Aural Comprehension—listening.
On the Michigan Test of English Language Proficiency—grammar, vocabulary, and reading.
On the Michigan Composition Test—writing.
These are the language skills that you will need to succeed in an academic course of studies.

What Is an Official Michigan Test?

An Official Michigan Test is a test that is graded at the University of Michigan.

You can take an Official Michigan Test at the University of Michigan or at another school that has permission from the University of Michigan to offer the Official Test. If you take an Official Test at another school, your teacher must send the test to the University of Michigan to be graded.

Official Tests are forms that are marked with letters from the second half of the alphabet, like M, N, and so on.

How Do I Register for an Official Michigan Test?

To register for an Official Michigan Test, your school must write to the University of Michigan at the following address to request that you be tested:

> Testing and Certification Office
> English Language Institute
> The University of Michigan
> North University Building
> Ann Arbor, Michigan 48104

What Is an <u>Un</u>official Michigan Test?

An Unofficial Michigan Test is a test that is not graded at the University of Michigan. Your teacher or advisor will probably grade your test at the school where you take it.

Unofficial Michigan Tests are forms that are marked with letters from the first half of the alphabet like A, B, C, D, E, F, G, and H.

How Do I Register for an <u>Un</u>official Michigan Test?

Each school has its own rules for registration. The foreign student advisor at the school that you want to attend is the best person to ask for information.

How Much Does It Cost to Register for the Michigan Test Battery?

The fee for the test is $15 in U.S. currency, or its equivalent in local currency, to be paid to the examiner before the test.

May I Register on the Day of the Test?

Registration for the Official Michigan Test is not permitted on the day of the examination. At some schools, registration for the Unofficial Michigan Test on the day of the examination is permitted under special circumstances.

You must also write a letter like the one below:

```
                                    (Write your address here)
                                    (Write the date here)



Testing and Certification Office
English Language Institute
The University of Michigan
North University Building
Ann Arbor, Michigan 48104


Dear Sir:


     Please send me the name and address of the Official

Michigan Test examiner in my area so that I can make an

appointment to be tested.

     (Write the name of your school here) has requested

that I submit a score.


                                    Sincerely yours,

                                    (Write your name here)
```

When the Testing and Certification Office at the University of Michigan receives a letter from your school, as well as your letter, they will send you the name and address of the examiner in your area. You must then make arrangements with the examiner to be tested.

What Should I Take with Me to the Test Room?

Take your passport and three sharpened number two pencils with erasers on them. It would be very helpful to take a watch. Books, dictionaries, tape recorders, and notes are not permitted in the test room.

Where Should I Sit?

If you can choose your own seat, try to locate the speakers attached to the tape recorder that will be used in the Michigan Test of Aural Comprehension. Remember, even though the tape recorder is in the front of the room, the speakers may be set up in the back of the room. Choose a seat near the speakers, but not directly in front of them. If a tape recorder is not used, try to sit in the center section of the room, not on the sides. The examiner will probably stand in front in the center of the room, and his or her voice will be clearest and loudest in the center section.

If you cannot choose your own seat, don't worry. It is the responsibility of the examiner to ensure that everyone is able to hear. If you can't hear well, ask the examiner to adjust the volume on the tape recorder or to speak more loudly.

What Should I Do If I Arrive Late?

If you arrive late, you will probably find the door to the test room locked. The Michigan Test Battery usually begins on time, and students who arrive late are not permitted to enter the room.

If you arrive late and find the door locked, call or go to the office where you registered for the test. Ask for advice.

How Long Is the Testing Session for the Michigan Test Battery?

See *Timetable*, page xii.

How Do I Answer the Test Questions?

Read the possible answers in your test book and mark the corresponding space on your answer sheet.

How Do I Mark the Answer Sheet?

There are sample questions in this book for each test in the Michigan Test Battery. Mark your answer sheet the same way that it is marked for the sample questions.

Because it takes a little longer to finish an examination when you mark the answer on a separate sheet, always practice using the answer sheets when you take the timed model tests in this book.

Before the test begins, the examiner will explain how to mark the answer sheet. He or she will remind you to fill in the spaces completely.

May I Erase an Answer?

You may erase an answer if you do it carefully and completely. Stray pencil marks may cause inaccurate scoring.

If I Am Not Sure of an Answer, Should I Guess?

If you are not sure of an answer, you should guess. The number of incorrect answers is not subtracted from your score. Your score is based upon the number of correct answers only.

Do not mark more than one answer for any question. Do not leave any questions blank on your answer sheet.

How Should I Guess?

First, eliminate all of the possibilities which you know are not correct. Then, if you are almost sure of an answer, guess that one.

If you have no idea of the correct answer for a question, choose one letter and use it for your "guess" answer throughout the entire test.

By using the same letter each time that you guess, you will probably answer correctly about 25 percent of the time. This percentage is usually better than the percentage of correct answers obtained by random guessing.

The "guess" answer is especially useful for finishing a test quickly. If the examiner tells you to stop working on one of the tests before you have finished it, answer all of the remaining questions with your "guess" answer.

What Should I Do If I Discover That I Have Marked My Answer Sheet Incorrectly?

Do not panic. Notify the examiner immediately.

If you have marked one answer in the wrong space on the answer sheet, the rest of the answers will be out of sequence. Ask for time at the end of the test to correct the sequence. If you have marked the answers in the test book instead of on the answer sheet, ask to have your test book attached to your answer sheet.

To avoid mismarking and to save space on your desk, use your test book as a marker on your answer sheet. As you advance, slide the book down underneath the number of the question that you are marking on the answer sheet. This is especially important on the Michigan Test of Aural Comprehension, where you may be looking up at the examiner, then down at your answer sheet. Be careful.

If I Score Very Poorly on One of the Tests, Is It Still Possible to Receive a Good Total Score on the Michigan Test Battery?

If you have mismarked one of the tests or if you feel that you have done very poorly on one of the tests, do not despair. You may receive a low score on one of the tests and still receive a good total score on the Michigan Test Battery if your scores on the other tests are good.

How Are the Tests Scored?

Each test is given a *raw score* and a *converted* or *equated score*. The raw score is the total number of questions that you answered correctly. The converted or equated score is the total number of points that you received for your correct answers. For example, 60 correct answers may be worth 80 points. In this case, the raw score would be 60. The converted or equated score would be 80.

How Do I Interpret My Scores?

Your total score is the average of the converted or equated scores for all of the tests that you take in the Michigan Test Battery.

There are no passing or failing scores on the Michigan Test Battery. Each school will evaluate the scores according to its own requirements. Even at the same university, the requirements may vary for different programs of study.

The admissions policies summarized below are typical of American universities, assuming, of course, that the applicant's other qualifications are acceptable.

Michigan Test Battery Score	Admissions Policy
85 or higher	Admission assured.
80-85	Admission probable.
70-80	Individual cases reviewed. Part-time admission possible for programs at some universities.
65-70	Individual cases reviewed; part-time admission possible for some technical or two-year programs.
65 or lower	More English study required.

When Will I Receive My Score Report?

If you take an Official Michigan Test, you will receive your score in the mail from the Testing and Certification Office at the University of Michigan in six weeks or less. If you take an Unofficial Michigan Test, you will receive your score from your teacher or advisor in two weeks or less.

How Will the Agencies Or Universities of My Choice Be Informed of My Score?

If you take an Official Michigan Test, the Testing and Certification Office at the University of Michigan will send your score to the school or schools that requested you be tested. If you take an Unofficial Michigan Test, you should ask the examiner to send your score to the school or schools that you may want to attend.

Is the Validity of a Score the Same for Both the Official and the Unofficial Tests?

Yes. The Official Test and the Unofficial Test are of the same difficulty. But some schools require Official Test scores.

　　You should find out whether the school that you want to attend will accept an Unofficial Test score before you take an Unofficial Michigan Test.

Are All Sections of the Test Always Given?

Sometimes an interview will be given instead of the Michigan Test of Aural Comprehension. It will consist of a five- or ten-minute conversation in English about your plans. You will be asked to answer questions about why you came to the United States, where you want to study, what your major field of study will be, and what you plan to do when you return to your native country.

　　Sometimes only the Michigan Test of English Language Proficiency will be given.

May I Take the Michigan Test Battery More Than Once?

You may take the Michigan Test Battery three times in any year. But you may not take the Test Battery more than once in a six-week period.

If I Have Already Taken the Michigan Test Battery, How Will the First Score or Scores Affect the New Score?

The school that receives the score reports will probably consider only your most recent score. Some schools will consider only your highest score, whether or not it is the most recent score.

Is There a Direct Correspondence Between a Score on the Test of English as a Foreign Language (TOEFL) and a Score on the Michigan Test Battery?

Most studies show a direct correspondence between a score on the TOEFL and a score on the Michigan Test Battery. A student who receives a score of 500 on the TOEFL will usually receive a score near 80 on the Michigan Test Battery.

How Is the Michigan Test Battery Like the Test of English as a Foreign Language?

The Michigan Test Battery is like the TOEFL in two ways:

(1) *The purpose*. They are both used to evaluate English proficiency, to assist in placement, and to measure progress.

(2) *The language skills tested*. They both test listening, structure, vocabulary, reading, and composition.

How Is the Michigan Test Battery Different from the Test of English as a Foreign Language?

The Michigan Test Battery is different from the TOEFL in three ways:

(1) *The types of listening comprehension problems tested*. The Test of Aural Comprehension in the Michigan Test Battery is similar to the questions and statements in Part A of the Listening Comprehension Section of the TOEFL. But the Test of Aural Comprehension does not have conversations and mini-talks like those in Parts B and C of the Listening Comprehension Section of the TOEFL.

(2) *The types of reading passages tested*. The Michigan Test of English Language Proficiency has one-paragraph reading passages similar to those found in textbooks and similar to some of those found in the Vocabulary and Reading Comprehension Section of the TOEFL. But the MTELP does not have one-sentence reading passages or short reading passages from newspapers, bulletins, and labels like some of those found in the Vocabulary and Reading Section of the TOEFL.

(3) *The type of composition test used*. The Michigan Composition Test requires you to choose one of two or three topics and then plan and write a one-page composition about it. But the Structure and Written Expression Section of the TOEFL has twenty-five sentences with errors to identify. The TOEFL requires no writing.

Is the Michigan Test Battery More Difficult than the Test of English as a Foreign Language?

Some students say that the TOEFL is more difficult. Usually they are students who have problems with listening comprehension. The TOEFL has a longer listening comprehension section than the Michigan Test Battery does.

Other students say that the Michigan Test Battery is more difficult. Usually they are students who have problems writing compositions. The Michigan Test Battery has a test in which the student must write a composition, but the TOEFL does not.

If a Student Speaks English Well, Will That Student Score Well on the Michigan Test Battery?

A student who speaks English well will not always score well on the Michigan Test Battery. The Michigan Test Battery is not a test of speaking. You may speak English very well and still not score well on the reading, vocabulary, grammar, and composition tests of the Michigan Test Battery. You need more than good speaking skills to succeed on the Michigan Test Battery because you need more than good speaking skills to succeed in a university class.

If a Student Speaks, Reads, Writes, and Understands English Structure, Will That Student Score Well on the Michigan Test Battery?

A student who speaks, reads, writes, and understands English structure will probably score well on the Michigan Test Battery. But there is not always a direct correspondence between proficiency in English and a good score. Many students who are proficient in English are not proficient in how to approach the Test Battery. That is why it is important to prepare by using this book.

Practicing Aural Comprehension

The Michigan Test
of Aural Comprehension

CHAPTER 2

The Michigan Test of Aural Comprehension

DESCRIPTION OF THE TEST

The Michigan Test of Aural Comprehension is a test of your ability to understand spoken English structures. It is a multiple-choice test with ninety problems.

There are three forms: Form 1, 2, and 3. All of the forms are at the same level of difficulty. The same test book is used for all of the forms. However, the problems for each form are different, and the answers that you choose—(a), (b), or (c)—will also be different for each form.

Don't try to remember answers from a test that you have already taken. The answer that you are remembering could be from a different form.

The problems are *questions* or short *statements*. Some examiners will play a tape containing the problems; other examiners will read the problems to you. You will notice that the vocabulary is very easy, but the structures may be difficult. You should listen carefully to the structures in each question or statement.

The total time for the test is about twenty-five minutes.

Answer Sheet—Aural Comprehension
Model Test One

Name _____ Date _____

	a	b	c		a	b	c		a	b	c
1.	( )	( )	( )	25.	( )	( )	( )	49.	( )	( )	( )
2.	( )	( )	( )	26.	( )	( )	( )	50.	( )	( )	( )
3.	( )	( )	( )	27.	( )	( )	( )	51.	( )	( )	( )
4.	( )	( )	( )	28.	( )	( )	( )	52.	( )	( )	( )
5.	( )	( )	( )	29.	( )	( )	( )	53.	( )	( )	( )
6.	( )	( )	( )	30.	( )	( )	( )	54.	( )	( )	( )
7.	( )	( )	( )	31.	( )	( )	( )	55.	( )	( )	( )
8.	( )	( )	( )	32.	( )	( )	( )	56.	( )	( )	( )
9.	( )	( )	( )	33.	( )	( )	( )	57.	( )	( )	( )
10.	( )	( )	( )	34.	( )	( )	( )	58.	( )	( )	( )
11.	( )	( )	( )	35.	( )	( )	( )	59.	( )	( )	( )
12.	( )	( )	( )	36.	( )	( )	( )	60.	( )	( )	( )

	a	b	c			a	b	c
73.	( )	( )	( )
74.	( )	( )	( )
75.	( )	( )	( )
76.	( )	( )	( )
77.	( )	( )	( )
78.	( )	( )	( )
79.	( )	( )	( )
80.	( )	( )	( )
81.	( )	( )	( )

	a	b	c		a	b	c		a	b	c		a	b	c
13.	( )	( )	( )	37.	( )	( )	( )	61.	( )	( )	( )	82.	( )	( )	( )
14.	( )	( )	( )	38.	( )	( )	( )	62.	( )	( )	( )	83.	( )	( )	( )
15.	( )	( )	( )	39.	( )	( )	( )	63.	( )	( )	( )	84.	( )	( )	( )
16.	( )	( )	( )	40.	( )	( )	( )	64.	( )	( )	( )	85.	( )	( )	( )
17.	( )	( )	( )	41.	( )	( )	( )	65.	( )	( )	( )	86.	( )	( )	( )
18.	( )	( )	( )	42.	( )	( )	( )	66.	( )	( )	( )	87.	( )	( )	( )
19.	( )	( )	( )	43.	( )	( )	( )	67.	( )	( )	( )	88.	( )	( )	( )
20.	( )	( )	( )	44.	( )	( )	( )	68.	( )	( )	( )	89.	( )	( )	( )
21.	( )	( )	( )	45.	( )	( )	( )	69.	( )	( )	( )	90.	( )	( )	( )
22.	( )	( )	( )	46.	( )	( )	( )	70.	( )	( )	( )
23.	( )	( )	( )	47.	( )	( )	( )	71.	( )	( )	( )
24.	( )	( )	( )	48.	( )	( )	( )	72.	( )	( )	( )

Answer Sheet—Aural Comprehension
Model Test Two

Name _____ Date _____

	a	b	c		a	b	c		a	b	c		a	b	c
1.	( )	( )	( )	25.	( )	( )	( )	49.	( )	( )	( )				
2.	( )	( )	( )	26.	( )	( )	( )	50.	( )	( )	( )				
3.	( )	( )	( )	27.	( )	( )	( )	51.	( )	( )	( )		a	b	c
4.	( )	( )	( )	28.	( )	( )	( )	52.	( )	( )	( )	73.	( )	( )	( )
5.	( )	( )	( )	29.	( )	( )	( )	53.	( )	( )	( )	74.	( )	( )	( )
6.	( )	( )	( )	30.	( )	( )	( )	54.	( )	( )	( )	75.	( )	( )	( )
7.	( )	( )	( )	31.	( )	( )	( )	55.	( )	( )	( )	76.	( )	( )	( )
8.	( )	( )	( )	32.	( )	( )	( )	56.	( )	( )	( )	77.	( )	( )	( )
9.	( )	( )	( )	33.	( )	( )	( )	57.	( )	( )	( )	78.	( )	( )	( )
10.	( )	( )	( )	34.	( )	( )	( )	58.	( )	( )	( )	79.	( )	( )	( )
11.	( )	( )	( )	35.	( )	( )	( )	59.	( )	( )	( )	80.	( )	( )	( )
12.	( )	( )	( )	36.	( )	( )	( )	60.	( )	( )	( )	81.	( )	( )	( )

	a	b	c		a	b	c		a	b	c		a	b	c
13.	( )	( )	( )	37.	( )	( )	( )	61.	( )	( )	( )	82.	( )	( )	( )
14.	( )	( )	( )	38.	( )	( )	( )	62.	( )	( )	( )	83.	( )	( )	( )
15.	( )	( )	( )	39.	( )	( )	( )	63.	( )	( )	( )	84.	( )	( )	( )
16.	( )	( )	( )	40.	( )	( )	( )	64.	( )	( )	( )	85.	( )	( )	( )
17.	( )	( )	( )	41.	( )	( )	( )	65.	( )	( )	( )	86.	( )	( )	( )
18.	( )	( )	( )	42.	( )	( )	( )	66.	( )	( )	( )	87.	( )	( )	( )
19.	( )	( )	( )	43.	( )	( )	( )	67.	( )	( )	( )	88.	( )	( )	( )
20.	( )	( )	( )	44.	( )	( )	( )	68.	( )	( )	( )	89.	( )	( )	( )
21.	( )	( )	( )	45.	( )	( )	( )	69.	( )	( )	( )	90.	( )	( )	( )
22.	( )	( )	( )	46.	( )	( )	( )	70.	( )	( )	( )				
23.	( )	( )	( )	47.	( )	( )	( )	71.	( )	( )	( )				
24.	( )	( )	( )	48.	( )	( )	( )	72.	( )	( )	( )				

Answer Sheet—Aural Comprehension
Model Test Three

Name _____ Date _____

	a	b	c			a	b	c			a	b	c			a	b	c
1.	( )	( )	( )		25.	( )	( )	( )		49.	( )	( )	( )					
2.	( )	( )	( )		26.	( )	( )	( )		50.	( )	( )	( )					
3.	( )	( )	( )		27.	( )	( )	( )		51.	( )	( )	( )					
4.	( )	( )	( )		28.	( )	( )	( )		52.	( )	( )	( )		73.	( )	( )	( )
5.	( )	( )	( )		29.	( )	( )	( )		53.	( )	( )	( )		74.	( )	( )	( )
6.	( )	( )	( )		30.	( )	( )	( )		54.	( )	( )	( )		75.	( )	( )	( )
7.	( )	( )	( )		31.	( )	( )	( )		55.	( )	( )	( )		76.	( )	( )	( )
8.	( )	( )	( )		32.	( )	( )	( )		56.	( )	( )	( )		77.	( )	( )	( )
9.	( )	( )	( )		33.	( )	( )	( )		57.	( )	( )	( )		78.	( )	( )	( )
10.	( )	( )	( )		34.	( )	( )	( )		58.	( )	( )	( )		79.	( )	( )	( )
11.	( )	( )	( )		35.	( )	( )	( )		59.	( )	( )	( )		80.	( )	( )	( )
12.	( )	( )	( )		36.	( )	( )	( )		60.	( )	( )	( )		81.	( )	( )	( )

	a	b	c			a	b	c			a	b	c			a	b	c
13.	( )	( )	( )		37.	( )	( )	( )		61.	( )	( )	( )		82.	( )	( )	( )
14.	( )	( )	( )		38.	( )	( )	( )		62.	( )	( )	( )		83.	( )	( )	( )
15.	( )	( )	( )		39.	( )	( )	( )		63.	( )	( )	( )		84.	( )	( )	( )
16.	( )	( )	( )		40.	( )	( )	( )		64.	( )	( )	( )		85.	( )	( )	( )
17.	( )	( )	( )		41.	( )	( )	( )		65.	( )	( )	( )		86.	( )	( )	( )
18.	( )	( )	( )		42.	( )	( )	( )		66.	( )	( )	( )		87.	( )	( )	( )
19.	( )	( )	( )		43.	( )	( )	( )		67.	( )	( )	( )		88.	( )	( )	( )
20.	( )	( )	( )		44.	( )	( )	( )		68.	( )	( )	( )		89.	( )	( )	( )
21.	( )	( )	( )		45.	( )	( )	( )		69.	( )	( )	( )		90.	( )	( )	( )
22.	( )	( )	( )		46.	( )	( )	( )		70.	( )	( )	( )					
23.	( )	( )	( )		47.	( )	( )	( )		71.	( )	( )	( )					
24.	( )	( )	( )		48.	( )	( )	( )		72.	( )	( )	( )					

MODEL TESTS ONE, TWO, AND THREE AURAL COMPREHENSION

90 Questions

25 Minutes

Directions

This is a test of your ability to understand spoken English structure. There are ninety problems in each test, with three possible answers for each problem. You will hear either a question or a statement. When you hear a question, read the three possible answers, (a), (b), and (c). (At the official test you will be given a test book with these answer choices.) Choose the one that would be the best answer to the question. When you hear a statement, read the three possible answers, (a), (b), and (c). Choose the one that would be the closest in meaning to the statement that you have heard. These questions and statements will not be repeated. You have 12 seconds to select and mark your answer.

> Note that there is only *one* set of answer choices for Model Tests One, Two, and Three. (This follows the pattern of the actual test which uses the same test book for these three test forms.) Therefore, use the available cassette of tests one, two, and three, listen to the problems for whichever model test you select, choose your answers from the choices that follow, tear out the answer sheet and mark your answers. Remember, you will use the same set of answer choices for each of the three tests. Each test covers different principles and requires different answers. The transcript in the Appendix of this book corresponds to the tests on the cassette. If you use the transcript (pages 179-190) instead of the cassette to take the tests, you must have an English-speaking person read the questions and statements, pausing for 12 seconds between each item.

SAMPLE TEST ITEMS: QUESTIONS

Form 1	Form 2	Form 3
You will hear:	**You will hear:**	**You will hear:**
1. Did John give you the message in time?	1. Did Mary give you the message in time?	1. Did the message arrive in time?
You will read:	**You will read:**	**You will read:**
1. a. Yes, he did. b. Yes, she did. c. Yes, it did.	1. a. Yes, he did. b. Yes, she did. c. Yes, it did.	1. a. Yes, he did. b. Yes, she did. c. Yes, it did.
You should mark:	**You should mark:**	**You should mark:**

1. a   b   c
   (x) ( ) ( )
	1. a b c
	   ( ) (x) ( )
		1. a b c
		   ( ) ( ) (x)

SAMPLE TEST ITEMS: STATEMENTS

Form 1	Form 2	Form 3
You will hear:	**You will hear:**	**You will hear:**
2. Bill can't meet you at the airport, but I can.	2. Bill can't meet you at the airport, and I can't either.	2. Bill can meet you at the airport, and I can too.
You will read:	**You will read:**	**You will read:**
2. a. Only I can meet you. b. Neither Bill nor I can meet you. c. Both Bill and I can meet you.	2. a. Only I can meet you. b. Neither Bill nor I can meet you. c. Both Bill and I can meet you.	2. a. Only I can meet you. b. Neither Bill nor I can meet you. c. Both Bill and I can meet you.
You should mark:	**You should mark:**	**You should mark:**

2. a   b   c
   (x) ( ) ( )
	2. a b c
	   ( ) (x) ( )
		2. a b c
		   ( ) ( ) (x)

Now select the test you wish to hear, turn to the next page for the answer choices, and begin the test. Remember, you will be given 25 minutes for each test. Time yourself.

Answer Choices: Model Tests One, Two, and Three

1. a. Yes, they have.
    b. Yes, they are.
    c. Yes, they will.

2. a. Yes, I am.
    b. Yes, she is.
    c. Yes, it is.

3. a. I went only to the movie.
    b. I read only the book
    c. I read the book and saw the movie.

4. a. We have quite a lot of snow in February.
    b. We occasionally have snow in February.
    c. We don't have any snow in February.

5. a. The buses begin running at eight o'clock.
    b. The buses don't begin running at eight o'clock.
    c. The buses end the run at eight o'clock.

6. a. So John wrote it.
    b. So Alice wrote it.
    c. So I wrote it.

7. a. I studied at State University.
    b. I studied at City College.
    c. I studied at Community College.

8. a. The orchestra never played professionally.
    b. The orchestra played more professionally before.
    c. The orchestra played more professionally than ever.

9. a. Yes, he is.
    b. Yes, she is.
    c. Yes, it is.

10. a. No, I still have a few.
    b. No, I still have a little.
    c. Yes, I have some.

11. a. The police arrested Mabel.
    b. The police arrested Tom and me.
    c. The police arrested Tom.

12. a. Two hundred dollars.
    b. Only two of them.
    c. Twice.

13. a. No, they haven't.
    b. No, they didn't.
    c. No, it hasn't.

14. a. Next week.
    b. Yes, she is.
    c. Yes, it is.

15. a. We received her letter after Tom had called her.
    b. Despite our receiving her letter, Tom called her.
    c. Because of her letter, Tom called her.

16. a. No, he isn't.
    b. No, it isn't.
    c. No, she isn't.

17. a. Joe wanted a lot to eat.
    b. Joe didn't want much to eat.
    c. Joe didn't want anything to eat.

18. a. Yes, they are.
    b. Yes, he is.
    c. Yes, it is.

19. a. Both are his.
    b. One of them is his.
    c. Neither is his.

20. a. They left during the classes.
    b. They left after the classes.
    c. They left before the classes.

21. a. I dropped it.
    b. Yes, I was.
    c. Yes, I did.

22. a. Yes, he was.
    b. Yes, she was.
    c. At Betty's house.

23. a. Yes, it is, thank you.
    b. Yes, it does, thank you.
    c. Yes, I will, thank you.

24. a. Anne is.
    b. Yes, she js.
    c. A patient person.

25. a. I'll remember it.
    b. I'll remember him.
    c. He'll remember me.

26. a. Yes, I was.
    b. Yes, it is.
    c. Yes, she is.

27. a. She knew when the baby would come.
    b. She didn't know when the doctor would come.
    c. She thought the doctor knew when it would come.

28. a. Yes, it did.
    b. Yes, I did.
    c. I passed it.

29. a. He won't go.
    b. He will go.
    c. He may go.

30. a. No, it wasn't.
    b. No, she wasn't.
    c. No, he wasn't.

31. a. Our neighbors were friendlier before.
    b. Our neighbors are friendlier now than before.
    c. Our neighbors are not friendly.

32. a. They'll get them.
    b. He'll get it for her.
    c. She'll get it for him.

33. a. Someone helped the foreign student advisor and the students.
    b. The students helped the foreign student advisor.
    c. The foreign student advisor helped the students.

34. a. In the main office.
    b. To the main office.
    c. To manage the main office.

35. a. I arrived after the cake had been cut.
    b. I arrived before the cake had been cut.
    c. I arrived while the cake was being cut.

36. a. Yes, it is.
    b. Yes, he is.
    c. Yes, they did.

37. a. Yes, they do.
    b. Dr. Anderson.
    c. On the next floor.

38. a. She planned to go winter quarter.
    b. She planned to come back winter quarter.
    c. She didn't plan to go winter quarter.

39. a. Yes, she is.
    b. Yes, it is.
    c. Yes, they are.

40. a. You visited it.
    b. You visited them.
    c. They visited you.

41. a. I believe she would have.
    b. I believe she would.
    c. I believe she has.

42. a. Yes, they do.
    b. Yes, I do.
    c. Yes, it does.

43. a. Yes, there was.
    b. Yes, there were.
    c. Yes, it was.

44. a. James thought that I knew what would happen.
    b. James knew what would happen.
    c. James didn't know what would happen.

45. a. The World Cup Soccer Championship.
    b. Soccer games.
    c. All of the time.

46. a. It began on the afternoon of the wedding.
     b. It ended on the afternoon of the wedding.
     c. It didn't begin on the afternoon of the wedding.

47. a. They thought that I knew where it was parked.
     b. They knew where it was parked.
     c. We didn't know where it was parked.

48. a. A large state university.
     b. To State University.
     c. From State University.

49. a. We might live there.
     b. We must live there.
     c. We should live there.

50. a. No, he wasn't.
     b. It was our fault.
     c. It wasn't our fault.

51. a. Bill is.
     b. Bill does.
     c. For Bill.

52. a. Much better.
     b. Playing baseball.
     c. The right one.

53. a. Turn left at the first light.
     b. 915 S Street.
     c. 877-9891.

54. a. Several hundred dollars.
     b. An electric one.
     c. The smaller one.

55. a. Yes, I could.
     b. Yes, I could have.
     c. Yes, I have.

56. a. Yes, it has.
     b. Yes, she has.
     c. Yes, it is.

57. a. UCLA won.
     b. The University of Southern California won.
     c. Neither team won.

58. a. Yes, I have a little.
     b. No, I have some.
     c. Yes, I have a few.

59. a. I know that they had some problems.
     b. I didn't know about the problems that they had.
     c. I don't think that they had any problems.

60. a. Yes, he could.
     b. Yes, he could have.
     c. Yes, he has.

61. a. All of our teachers are from the United States.
     b. None of our teachers is from the United States.
     c. One of our teachers is not from the United States.

62. a. No, thank you. I still have a few.
     b. No, thank you. I still have a little.
     c. No, I don't like to.

63. a. I'm going to tell her.
     b. Both Bill and I are going to tell her.
     c. Neither Bill nor I am going to tell her.

64. a. My girl friend is.
     b. My girl friend did.
     c. To my girl friend.

65. a. Yes, it did.
     b. Yes, I did.
     c. Yes, he did.

66. a. John is sicker than usual now.
     b. John is better than he was.
     c. John doesn't get sick.

67. a. Only Bill is graduating.
     b. Both Bill and his cousin are graduating.
     c. Neither Bill nor his cousin is graduating.

68. a. Yes, they do.
     b. Yes, I do.
     c. Yes, it does.

69.   a. Yes, they do.
      b. Yes, it is.
      c. Yes, it does.

70.   a. I approve of Mr. Johnson.
      b. Yes, I think so.
      c. He'll probably give them away.

71.   a. She doesn't finish at five o'clock.
      b. She finishes at five o'clock.
      c. She'll start at five o'clock.

72.   a. Ten of them.
      b. Ten dollars.
      c. Once.

73.   a. Seats for the movie are not available.
      b. Seats for the movie are available.
      c. These are the correct seats.

74.   a. We must attend.
      b. We can't attend.
      c. We attended.

75.   a. A formal party dress.
      b. At a formal party.
      c. To a formal party.

76.   a. I took an efficiency.
      b. I took a one-bedroom.
      c. I took a two-bedroom.

77.   a. So I waited.
      b. So Mary waited.
      c. So the driver waited.

78.   a. It was all used.
      b. It wasn't used.
      c. It was only used in part.

79.   a. I was given only water.
      b. I was given only coffee.
      c. I was given both coffee and water.

80.   a. I bought the black coat.
      b. I bought the brown coat.
      c. I bought the red coat.

81.   a. To Mr. White.
      b. Mr. White is.
      c. Mr. White does.

82.   a. His wife didn't want him to smoke.
      b. His wife hadn't asked him not to smoke.
      c. His wife wanted to smoke.

83.   a. We stopped only in London.
      b. We stopped only in Paris.
      c. We stopped in both London and Paris.

84.   a. The teacher recommended it.
      b. You recommended the teacher.
      c. The teacher recommended you.

85.   a. To City College.
      b. Next year.
      c. Because my advisor told me to.

86.   a. One child doesn't go to nursery school.
      b. All of their children go to nursery school.
      c. None of their children goes to nursery school.

87.   a. I had to find my apartment.
      b. She had to find her apartment.
      c. John had to find his apartment.

88.   a. The doctor suggested that he keep working, and he did.
      b. The doctor suggested that he stop working, but he didn't.
      c. The doctor suggested that he keep working, but he didn't.

89.   a. So Mary and my roommate studied.
      b. So my roommate and I studied.
      c. So Mary and I studied.

90.   a. Fifteen dollars.
      b. Only two of them.
      c. Only once.

ANSWER KEYS AND EXPLANATORY ANSWERS AURAL COMPREHENSION

Model Test One

Answer Key

1.	b	19.	a	37.	b	55.	b	73.	a
2.	a	20.	b	38.	c	56.	b	74.	b
3.	c	21.	a	39.	c	57.	c	75.	a
4.	a	22.	a	40.	c	58.	a	76.	a
5.	c	23.	c	41.	c	59.	c	77.	c
6.	a	24.	b	42.	c	60.	a	78.	b
7.	b	25.	a	43.	a	61.	a	79.	b
8.	c	26.	b	44.	c	62.	c	80.	c
9.	a	27.	a	45.	b	63.	c	81.	b
10.	a	28.	b	46.	a	64.	c	82.	a
11.	b	29.	a	47.	a	65.	c	83.	b
12.	b	30.	c	48.	b	66.	c	84.	b
13.	c	31.	a	49.	a	67.	a	85.	b
14.	b	32.	b	50.	b	68.	a	86.	a
15.	a	33.	a	51.	b	69.	a	87.	b
16.	b	34.	a	52.	a	70.	c	88.	b
17.	b	35.	a	53.	a	71.	a	89.	a
18.	a	36.	c	54.	c	72.	c	90.	a

Explanatory Answers

1. **b** The auxiliary *are* must be used in the answer to refer to the auxiliary *are* used in the question.

2. **a** The auxiliary *am* and the pronoun *I* must be used in the answer to refer to the auxiliary *are* and the pronoun *you* used in the question. Remember, *I* or *we* is a correct response to a question with the pronoun *you*.

3. **c** *Both* "the book" and "the movie" must be mentioned in the answer when the inclusive adverb *also* is used in the statement. Remember, *also* means *in addition to*.

4. **a** Because "it *usually* snows in February," it must be concluded that "we have *quite a lot* of snow." Remember, *usually* means *a lot*.

5. **c** Because "the buses *don't stop* running *until* eight o'clock," it must be concluded that "[they] *end* the run at eight o'clock." Remember, the preposition *until* means *before*.

6. **a** Because the speaker "told *John* to write the paper," it must be concluded that "*John* wrote it."

7. **b** Because the speaker says he "decided to study at *City College*," it must be concluded that he studied there. He gives reasons for *not* studying at State University or at Community College.

8. **c** Because "I've *never* heard the orchestra play *more* professionally," it must be concluded that "the orchestra played *more* professionally *than ever*." Remember, *never more* means *more than ever*.

9. **a** The masculine pronoun *he* must be used in the answer to refer to the masculine name *Bob* used in the question.

10. **a** The adjective phrase *a few* must be used in the answer to refer to the plural count noun *oranges* used in the question. Although *some* may be used with either a plural count noun or a non-count noun, choice (c) is not a logical response to the question. Because the speaker says "I *have* some," it is not logical for him to say *yes* in response to the question, "Shall I *buy* some?"

11. **b** "Tom and I were arrested by the police" is a passive form of the active statement, "The police arrested Tom and me." Mabel was *surprised,* not *arrested*.

12. **b** The quantity number *two* must be used in the answer to refer to the count noun *students* in the question, "How many *students*?" Choice (a) refers to *money* and choice (c) refers to *time*, not *students*.

13. **c** The auxiliary *hasn't* and the singular pronoun *it* must be used in the answer to refer to the auxiliary *has* and the singular noun *letter* used in the question.

14. **b** The auxiliary *is* and the feminine pronoun *she* must be used in the answer to refer to the auxiliary *is* and feminine name *Ruth* used in the question.

15. **a** Because "Tom called her before we received her letter," it must be concluded that "we received her letter after Tom had called her." In both statements, the same chronological order occurs.

16. **b** The neuter pronoun *it* must be used in the answer to refer to the neuter noun phrase *phone number* used in the question.

17. **b** Because "Joe was*n't very* hungry," it must be concluded that "[he] did*n't* want *much* to eat." Remember, *not very* means *not much* or *a little bit*.

18. **a** The plural pronoun *they* must be used in the answer to refer to the plural name *Williams's* used in the question. *Williams's* includes all of the members of the Williams family.

19. **a** *Both* must be mentioned in the answer when the affirmative adverb *so* is used in the statement. Remember, *so* means *also*.

20. **b** Because "Bill and Betty did*n't leave until* classes were *over* on Friday," it must be concluded that "they left *after* the classes." Remember, *over* means *finished*.

21. **a** In the answer a choice must be made between the two possibilities mentioned, "finish" *or* "drop," since the alternative conjunction *or* is used in the question.

22. a The auxiliary *was* and the masculine pronoun *he* must be used in the answer to refer to the auxiliary *wasn't* and the masculine pronoun *he* used in the tag question. Remember, a tag question is a short question at the end of a sentence. Negative tags usually assume an affirmative response.

23. c The auxiliary *will* and the pronoun *I* must be used in the answer to refer to the auxiliary *will* and the pronoun *you* used in the question. Remember, *I* or *we* is a correct response to a question with the pronoun *you*.

24. b The auxiliary *is* and the feminine pronoun *she* must be used in the answer to refer to the auxiliary *is* and the feminine noun *woman* used in the question.

25. a The neuter pronoun *it* must be used in the answer to refer to the neuter noun *day* used in the statement.

26. b The auxiliary *is* and the pronoun *it* must be used in the answer to refer to the auxilary *is* and the pronoun *it* used in the question, "*Is it* correct?"

27. a Because "*Ruth told* her doctor when the baby was due," it must be concluded that "*she knew* when the baby would come."

28. b The auxiliary *did* and the pronoun *I* must be used in the answer to refer to the auxiliary *did* and the pronoun *you* used in the question. Remember, *I* or *we* is a correct response to a question with the pronoun *you*.

29. a Because the speaker says "[he] will *not be able* to go see it [the game]," it must be concluded that "he *won't* go." Remember, *not able* means *can't*.

30. c The auxiliary *wasn't* and the masculine pronoun *he* must be used in the answer to refer to the auxiliary *wasn't* and the masculine noun *husband* used in the question.

31. a Because "our neighbors *have been friendlier* [in the past]," it must be concluded that "[they] *were friendlier* [before]."

32. b "Anna's certificate will be given [by someone] to her husband" is a passive form of the active statement, "Someone will give Anna's certificate to her husband." Because "someone will give it *to him*," it must be concluded that "*he'll* get it."

33. a "The students and the foreign student advisor were helped [by someone]" is a passive form of the active statement, "Someone helped the foreign student advisor and the students."

34. a A preposition of stationary location must be used in the answer when the word *where* is used with a form of *be* in the question. Remember, *stationary* means *not moving*. The prepositions *in, on, at, beside, between,* and *behind* are stationary prepositions.

35. a Because "she'*d just finished* cutting the cake when I arrived," it must be concluded that "I arrived *after* the cake had been cut." In both statements, the same chronological order occurs.

36. c The auxiliary *did* and the plural pronoun *they* must be used in the answer to refer to the auxiliary *did* and the two people, *Philip and Jane,* named in the question.

37. b A person must be mentioned in the answer when the word *who* is used in the question. Remember, *who* refers to people. When a statement is followed by a question, the correct answer refers to the question, not the statement.

38. c Because the speaker says "Linda *wasn't going to* go home winter quarter," it must be concluded that "she *didn't plan* to go." Remember, *not going to* means *not planning to* when it is used with *was* or *were*.

39. c The auxiliary *are* and the plural pronoun *they* must be used in the answer to refer to the auxiliary *are* and the plural name *Brown's* used in the question. *Brown's* includes all of the members of the Brown family.

40. c The plural pronoun *they* must be used in the answer to refer to the collective noun *family* used in the statement. Remember, a collective noun like *family* is plural when the individual members are considered. "The family [members] visited you."

41. c The auxiliary *has* must be used in the answer to refer to the auxiliary *has* used in the question.

42. c The auxiliary *does* and the pronoun *it* must be used in the answer to refer to the auxiliary *does* and the pronoun *it* used in the question.

43. a The auxiliary *was* and the subject *there* must be used in the answer to refer to the auxiliary *was* and the subject *there* used in the question.

44. c Because "James *wondered*," it must be concluded that "he *didn't know*." Remember, to *wonder* means to *be uncertain*.

45. b An indefinite description must be used in the answer when the phrase *what kind* is used in the question. *Soccer games* is indefinite because there is no reference to any definite game.

46. a Because the speaker says "it *didn't start* raining *until* the afternoon of the wedding" it must be concluded that "it *began* [raining] on the afternoon of the wedding." Remember, the preposition *until* means *before*.

47. a Because "they *asked me* where the car was parked," it must be concluded that "they thought that *I knew*."

48. b A preposition of directional location must be used in the answer when the word *where* is used with a verb of motion in the question. Remember, *send* is a verb of motion. The prepositions *to*, *down*, *up*, and *across* are directional prepositions.

49. a Because the speaker says "we'll *probably not* go there to live," it must be concluded that "we *might* live there." Remember, both *may* and *might* mean *probably*, but *might* means *less probably* and *may* means *more probably*.

50. b The speaker says "it was our fault."

51. b The name *Bill* and the auxiliary *does* must be used in the answer to refer to the question word *who* and the verb *works* used in the question. Remember, the auxiliaries *do*, *does*, and *did* are used to refer to all verbs except *be*.

52. a When the word *how* is used with a form of *be* in the question, an explanation of conditions or health must be given in the answer.

53. a Directions or explanations must be given in the answer when the word *how* is used in the question. Remember, when a statement is followed by a question, the correct answer refers to the question, not the statement.

54. c A definite description must be used in the answer when the word *which* is used in the question. Remember, an adjective phrase with the definite article *the* is a correct response to questions that require definite answers.

55. b The auxiliary *could have* must be used in the answer to refer to the auxiliary *couldn't have* used in the question.

56. b The auxiliary *has* and the pronoun *she* must be used in the answer to refer to the auxiliary *hasn't* and the pronoun *she* used in the tag question. Remember, a tag

question is a short question at the end of a sentence. Negative tags usually assume an affirmative response.

57. c Because the speaker says, "The University of Southern California and UCLA were *both beaten* [by other teams]," it must be concluded that "*neither* team *won*." Remember, to *beat* means to *win a victory over*.

58. a The adjective phrase *a little* must be used in the answer to refer to the non-count noun *homework* used in the question. Although *some* may be used with either a plural count noun or a non-count noun, choice (b) is not a logical response to the question. Because the speaker says "I *have some*," it is not logical for him to say *no* in response to the question, "Do you *have any*?"

59. c Because the speaker says "they had *no* problems that I am aware of," it must be concluded that "I do*n't* think that they had *any* problems." Remember, *no* means *not any*.

60. a The auxiliary *could* must be used in the answer to refer to the auxiliary *could* used in the question.

61. a *All* must be mentioned in the answer to refer to the two negatives *no* and *not* used in the statement. Remember, two negative words in English often make a statement affirmative. "*No* teacher who's *not*" means "*all* teachers who are."

62. c The auxiliary *don't* and the pronoun *I* must be used in the answer to refer to the auxiliary *do* and the pronoun *you* used in the question. Remember, *I* or *we* is a correct response to a question with the pronoun *you*.

63. c *Neither* must be mentioned in the answer when *not either* is used in the statement. Remember, *neither* means *not either*.

64. c The preposition *to* must be used with a name in the answer when the preposition *to* is used with the question word *who* in the question.

65. c The masculine pronoun *he* must be used in the answer to refer to the masculine name *Al* used in the question.

66. c Because "John has *never* been sick," it must be concluded that "he does*n't* [ever] get sick." Remember, *never* means *not ever*.

67. a Only "Bill" must be mentioned in the answer when *isn't* is used with "cousin" in the statement.

68. a The plural pronoun *they* must be used in the answer to refer to the plural noun *girls* used in the question. Remember, *do* must be used for agreement between auxiliary and pronoun.

69. a The auxiliary *do* and the pronoun *they* must be used in the answer to refer to the auxiliary *do* and the collective noun *people* used in the question. Remember, a collective noun like *people* is plural, because the individual members are considered.

70. c An activity must be mentioned in the answer when *what* is used with the verb *do* in the question.

71. a Because "Miss Smith does*n't stop* practicing at five o'clock," it must be concluded that "she does*n't finish* at five o'clock." Remember, to *stop* means to *finish*.

72. c The frequency number *once* must be used in the answer to refer to the count noun *times* used in the question, "How many times?" Remember, the phrase *how many times* means *how often*.

73. a   Because the speaker says "there are *no* seats," it must be concluded that "seats . . . are *not* available." Remember, *no* means *not any*.

74. b   Because the speaker says "we *aren't able* to go," it must be concluded that "we *can't* attend." Remember, *not able* means *can't*.

75. a   A noun or noun phrase must be used in the answer when the question word *what* is used with a form of *be* in the question.

76. a   The speaker says "[he] took an *efficiency*." He gives reasons for *not* taking a one-bedroom or a two-bedroom.

77. c   Because "Mary told *the taxi driver* that he should wait," it must be concluded that "*the driver* waited."

78. b   Because "the workbook was*n't* used *at all*," it must be concluded that "it was*n't* used." Remember, *not at all* means *not any*.

79. b   Because the speaker says "the waitress didn't give me the water," it must be concluded that "[he] was given *only* coffee." He *asked* for both, but he was not *given* both.

80. c   The speaker says he "bought *the red* coat." He gives reasons for *not* buying the black one or the brown one.

81. b   The name *Mr. White* and the auxiliary *is* must be used in the answer to refer to the question word *who* and the auxiliary *is* used in the question. Remember, *who* refers to people.

82. a   Because "his wife asked him to [stop smoking]," it must be concluded that "[she] didn't want him to smoke."

83. b   Only "Paris" must be mentioned in the answer when the exclusive adverb *instead* is used with "Paris" in the statement. Remember, *instead* means *in place of*.

84. b   "The teacher whom you recommended" is a relative clause form of the statement, "you recommended the teacher."

85. b   A time must be mentioned in the answer when the word *when* is used in the question. Remember, when a statement is followed by a question, the correct answer refers to the question, not the statement.

86. a   Because the speaker says "*a child*," it must be concluded that "*one* child doesn't go." Remember, the article *a* means *one*.

87. b   Because the speaker says "John didn't help his sister find an apartment," it must be concluded that "she had to find her apartment [alone]." The speaker says he was *upset*; he does not say he *helped* her.

88. b   "John continued working" and "his doctor said [he should stop working]" are the two clauses in the statement, "John continued working in spite of what his doctor said."

89. a   Because "Mary told me she [Mary] would study with my roommate," it must be concluded that "Mary and my roommate studied."

90. a   An amount of money must be mentioned in the answer when the question phrase *how much* is used with the verb *cost* in the question.

Model Test Two

Answer Key

1.	a	19.	c	37.	c	55.	a	73.	b
2.	c	20.	c	38.	a	56.	c	74.	a
3.	a	21.	b	39.	a	57.	a	75.	b
4.	c	22.	b	40.	b	58.	c	76.	b
5.	a	23.	b	41.	a	59.	a	77.	b
6.	c	24.	c	42.	b	60.	c	78.	c
7.	a	25.	c	43.	b	61.	b	79.	a
8.	b	26.	c	44.	b	62.	b	80.	a
9.	c	27.	c	45.	a	63.	a	81.	a
10.	c	28.	c	46.	c	64.	b	82.	b
11.	a	29.	b	47.	c	65.	b	83.	c
12.	a	30.	b	48.	a	66.	a	84.	a
13.	b	31.	c	49.	b	67.	b	85.	a
14.	c	32.	c	50.	c	68.	c	86.	b
15.	b	33.	c	51.	a	69.	c	87.	a
16.	c	34.	b	52.	c	70.	b	88.	a
17.	a	35.	c	53.	b	71.	b	89.	b
18.	b	36.	b	54.	a	72.	a	90.	c

Explanatory Answers

1. **a** The auxiliary *have* must be used in the answer to refer to the auxiliary *have* used in the question.

2. **c** The auxiliary *is* and the pronoun *it* must be used in the answer to refer to the auxiliary *is* and the pronoun *this* used in the question.

3. **a** Only "the movie" must be mentioned in the answer when the exclusive adverb *instead* is used with "movie" in the statement. Remember, *instead* means *in place of*.

4. **c** Because "it doesn't snow *at all* in February," it must be concluded that "we don't have *any* snow." Remember, *not at all* means *not any*.

5. **a** Because "the buses *don't start* running *until* eight o'clock," it must be concluded that "[they] *begin* running at eight o'clock." Remember the preposition *until* means *before*.

6. c Because "Alice told *me* to write the paper," it must be concluded that "*I* wrote it." The paper is *for* John, not *by* John.

7. a Because the speaker says he "decided to study at *State University*," it must be concluded that he studied there. He gives reasons for *not* studying at City College or Community College.

8. b Because "*I've heard* the orchestra play *more* professionally [in the past]," it must be concluded that "*[they] played more* professionally before" than they are playing now.

9. c The neuter pronoun *it* must be used in the answer to refer to the neuter noun *line* used in the question.

10. c The adjective *some* must be used in the answer to refer to the non-count noun *fish* used in the question. Although the adjective phrase *a little* may be used with a non-count noun, choice (b) is not a logical response to the question. If the speaker says "I still *have a little*, it would not be logical for him to say *no* in response to the question, "Do you *have any?*"

11. a "Mabel was arrested by the police" is a passive form of the active statement, "The police arrested Mabel." Tom and I were *surprised*, not *arrested*.

12. a An amount of money must be mentioned in the answer when the question phrase *how much* is used with the verb *cost* in the question.

13. b The auxiliary *didn't* and the plural pronoun *they* must be used in the answer to refer to the auxiliary *did* and the plural noun *officials* used in the question.

14. c The auxiliary *is* and the neuter pronoun *it* must be used in the answer to refer to the auxiliary *is* and the neuter noun phrase *next week* used in the question.

15. b Because "Tom called her *in spite of our receiving* her letter," it must be concluded that "*despite our receiving* her letter, Tom called us." Remember, *in spite of* means *despite*.

16. c The feminine pronoun *she* must be used in the answer to refer to the feminine name *Mabel* used in the question.

17. a Because "Joe was *really* hungry," it must be concluded that "[he] wanted *a lot* to eat." Remember, *really* means *very* or *a lot*.

18. b The masculine pronoun *he* must be used in the answer to refer to the masculine name *William* used in the question.

19. c *Neither* must be mentioned in the answer when *not* is used with *either* in the statement. Remember *neither* means *not either*.

20. c The speaker says "Bill and Betty left *before* classes had started."

21. b The auxiliary *was* and the pronoun *I* must be used in the answer to refer to the auxiliary *weren't* and the pronoun *you* used in the tag question. Remember, *I* or *we* is a correct response to a question with the pronoun *you*. A tag question is a short question at the end of a sentence. Negative tags usually assume an affirmative response.

22. b The auxiliary *was* and the feminine pronoun *she* must be used in the answer to refer to the auxiliary *was* and the feminine name *Betty* used in the question.

23. b The auxiliary *does* and the neuter pronoun *it* must be used in the answer to refer to the auxiliary *does* and the neuter noun *tea* used in the question.

24. c An indefinite description must be used in the answer when the phrase *what kind* is used in the question. Remember, the indefinite articles *an* and *a* are used with adjectives in indefinite descriptions.

25. c The masculine pronoun *him* must be used in the answer to refer to the masculine noun *man* used in the statement.

26. c The auxiliary *is* and the pronoun *she* must be used in the answer to refer to the auxiliary *is* and the noun *secretary* used in the question. The pronoun *he* could also refer to the noun *secretary*.

27. c Because "Ruth *asked the doctor* when the baby was due," it must be concluded that "she thought *the doctor knew* when it would come."

28. c A choice must be made in the answer between the two possibilities mentioned, "pass" *or* "fail," when the alternative conjunction *or* is used in the question.

29. b Because the speaker says "[he *is*] *going to* see it [the game]," it must be concluded that "he *will* go." Remember, *going to* means *will*.

30. b The auxiliary *wasn't* and the feminine pronoun *she* must be used in the answer to refer to the auxiliary *wasn't* and the feminine noun *daughter*.

31. c Because "our neighbors have *never* been friendly," it must be concluded that "[they] are *not [ever]* friendly." Remember, *never* means *not ever*.

32. c "Jim's certificate will be given [by someone] to his wife" is a passive form of the active statement, "Someone will give Jim's certificate to his wife." Because "someone will give it *to her*," it must be concluded that "*she*'ll get it."

33. c "The students were helped by the foreign student advisor" is a passive form of the active statement, "The foreign student advisor helped the students."

34. b A preposition of directional location must be used in the answer when the word *where* is used with a verb of motion. Remember, *go* is a verb of motion. The prepositions *to*, *down*, *up*, and *across* are directional prepositions.

35. c Because "I arrived just *as* she was cutting the cake," it must be concluded that "I arrived *while* the cake was being cut." Remember, *as* means *while*.

36. b The auxiliary *is* and the masculine pronoun *he* must be used in the answer to refer to the auxiliary *is* and the masculine name *Philip* used in the question.

37. c When the word *where* is used in the question, a place must be mentioned in the answer. Remember, when a statement is followed by a question, the correct answer refers to the question, not the statement.

38. a Because the speaker says "Linda *wasn't going to* go home *until* winter quarter," it must be concluded that "she *planned* to go winter quarter." Remember, the preposition *until* means *before*.

39. a The auxiliary *is* and the feminine pronoun *she* must be used in the answer to refer to the auxiliary *is* and the feminine name *Mrs. Brown* used in the question.

40. c The pronoun *you* and the plural pronoun *them* must be used in the answer to refer to the pronoun *you* and the collective noun *family* used in the statement. Remember, a collective noun like *family* is plural when the individual members are considered. "You visited [the members of the family]."

41. a The auxiliary *would have* must be used in the answer to refer to the auxiliary *would have* used in the question.

42. b The auxiliary *do* and the pronoun *I* must be used in the answer to refer to the auxiliary *do* and the pronoun *you* used in the question. Remember, *I* or *we* is a correct response to a question with the pronoun *you*.

43. b   The auxiliary *were* and the subject *there* must be used in the answer to refer to the auxiliary *were* and the subject *there* used in the question.

44. b   Because "*James told* me," it must be concluded that "*[he] knew.*"

45. a   When the word *which* is used with *event* in the question, a definite event must be mentioned in the answer. Remember, an adjective phrase with the definite article *the* is a correct response to a question that requires a definite answer.

46. c   Because "it *didn't start* raining on the afternoon of the wedding," it must be concluded that "it *didn't begin* on the afternoon of the wedding." Remember, to *start* means to *begin*.

47. c   Because "we *wondered* where we had parked the car," it must be concluded that "we *didn't know*." Remember, to *wonder* means to *be uncertain*.

48. a   An indefinite description must be used in the answer when the phrase *what kind* is used in the question. Remember, the indefinite articles *an* and *a* are used with adjectives in indefinite descriptions.

49. b   Because the speaker says "we *have to* go there to live," it must be concluded that "we *must* live there." Remember, *have to* means *must*.

50. c   The speaker says "it wasn't our fault." It is James, *not* the speaker, who believes it to be our fault.

51. a   The name *Bill* and the auxiliary *is* must be used in the answer to refer to the question word *who* and the verb *is* used in the question. Remember, *who* refers to people.

52. c   A definite description must be used in the answer when the word *which* is used in the question. Remember, an adjective phrase with the definite article *the* is a correct response to a question that requires a definite answer.

53. b   A specific street number must be mentioned in the answer when the word *what* is used with *address* in the question. Remember, when a statement is followed by a question, the correct answer refers to the question, not the statement.

54. a   An amount of money must be mentioned in the answer when the question word *what* is used with the verb *cost* in the question.

55. a   The auxiliary *could* must be used in the answer to refer to the auxiliary *couldn't* used in the question.

56. c   The auxiliary *is* and the pronoun *it* must be used in the answer to refer to the auxiliary *isn't* and the pronoun *it* used in the tag question. Remember, a tag question is a short question at the end of a sentence. Negative tags usually assume an affirmative response.

57. a   "The University of Southern California was beaten by UCLA" is a passive form of the statement, "UCLA beat the University of Southern California." Remember, to *beat* means to *win a victory over*.

58. c   The adjective phrase *a few* must be used in the answer to refer to the plural count noun *exams* used in the question. Although *some* may be used with either a plural count noun or a non-count noun, choice (b) is not a logical response to the question. Because the speaker says "I *have* some," it would not be logical for him to say *no* in response to the question, "Do you *have* any?"

59. a   Because the speaker says "they had a few problems that I *am aware of,*" it must be

concluded that "I *know* that they had some problems." Remember, to *be aware* means to *know*.

60. **c** The auxiliary *has* must be used in the answer to refer to the auxiliary *has* used in the question.

61. **b** *None* must be used in the answer to refer to the negative adjective *no* used in the statement. Remember, *no* means *not one* or *none*.

62. **b** The adjective phrase *a little* must be used in the answer to refer to the non-count noun *tea* used in the question.

63. **a** Because the speaker says "I *will* [tell her]," it must be concluded that "[he *is*] *going to* tell her." Remember, *will* means *going to*.

64. **b** The auxiliary *did* must be used with a name in the answer to refer to the past verb *sold* and the question word *who* used in the question. Remember, the auxiliaries *do*, *does*, and *did* are used to refer to all verbs except *be*. *Who* refers to people.

65. **b** The pronoun *I* must be used in the answer to refer to the pronoun *you* used in the question. Remember, *I* or *we* is a correct response to a question with the pronoun *you*.

66. **a** Because "John has *never* been sicker [than he is now]," it must be concluded that "[he] is sick*er than usual* now." Remember, *never* sick*er* means sick*er than ever* before.

67. **b** *Both* must be mentioned in the answer when the affirmative adverb *so* is used in the statement. Remember, *so* means *also*.

68. **c** The neuter pronoun *it* must be used in the answer to refer to the neuter pronoun *it* used in the question. *Does* must be used for agreement between the auxiliary and the pronoun.

69. **c** The auxiliary *does* and the neuter pronoun *it* must be used in the answer to refer to the auxiliary *does* and the neuter noun *food* used in the question.

70. **b** *Yes* or *no* must be used in the answer when the auxiliary *will* is used in the question. *So* is used in place of the subject and verb, *Mr. Johnson will*.

71. **b** Because "Miss Smith doesn't *stop* practicing *until* five o'clock," it must be concluded that "she *finishes* at five o'clock." Remember, the preposition *until* means *before*.

72. **a** The quantity number *ten* must be used in the answer when the question phrase *how many* is used with the noun *students* in the question. Choice (b) refers to *money*, and choice (c) refers to *time*, not *students*.

73. **b** Because the speaker says there are seats *left*, it must be concluded that seats are *available*. Remember, *left* means *not used*.

74. **a** Because the speaker says "we *have to* go," it must be concluded that "we *must* attend." Remember, *have to* means *must*.

75. **b** A preposition of stationary location must be used in the answer when the word *where* is used with a form of *be* in the question. Remember, *stationary* means *not moving*. The prepositions *in*, *on*, *at*, *beside*, *between*, *behind* are stationary prepositions.

76. **b** The speaker says that he took a *one-bedroom*. He gives reasons for *not* taking an efficiency and a two-bedroom.

77. **b** Because "I told *Mary* that she should wait," it must be concluded that "[*she*] waited."

78. **c** Because "the workbook was*n't all* used," it must be concluded that it was "used *in part*." Remember, *not all* means *some*.

79. a   Only "the water" must be mentioned in the answer when the exclusive adverb *instead* is used with "water" in the statement. Remember, *instead* means *in place of*.

80. a   The speaker says he "bought *the black* coat." He gives reasons for *not* buying the red one and the brown one.

81. a   The preposition *to* must be used with a name in the answer when the preposition *to* is used with the question word *who* in the question.

82. b   Because "his wife hadn't asked him to [quit smoking]," it must be concluded that "his wife hadn't asked him not to smoke."

83. c   Both "London" and "Paris" must be mentioned in the answer when the inclusive adverb *too* is used in the statement. Remember, *too* means *also*.

84. a   "The course that the teacher recommended" is a relative clause form of the statement, "the teacher recommended [the course]."

85. a   A place must be mentioned in the answer when the word *where* is used in the question. Remember, when a statement is followed by a question, the correct answer refers to the question, not the statement.

86. b   *All* must be mentioned in the answer to refer to the two negatives *no* and *not* used in the statement. Remember, two negative words in English often make a statement affirmative. "*No* children who *don't* go" means "*All* children go."

87. a   Because the speaker says "John and his sister didn't help [him]," it must be concluded that the speaker "had to find his apartment [alone]." Remember, *me* and *I* are used to refer to the speaker.

88. a   "John continued working" and "his doctor had said he could [continue working]" are the two clauses in the statement, "John continued working because his doctor had said he could."

89. b   Because "my roommate told Mary he'd study *with me*," it must be concluded that "my roommate and *I* studied."

90. c   The frequency number *once* must be used in the answer when the question phrase *how many times* is used in the question. Remember, the phrase *how many times* means *how often*.

Model Test Three

Answer Key

1.	c	19.	b	37.	a	55.	c	73.	c
2.	b	20.	a	38.	b	56.	a	74.	c
3.	b	21.	c	39.	b	57.	b	75.	c
4.	b	22.	c	40.	a	58.	b	76.	c
5.	b	23.	a	41.	b	59.	b	77.	a
6.	b	24.	a	42.	a	60.	b	78.	a
7.	c	25.	b	43.	c	61.	c	79.	c
8.	a	26.	a	44.	a	62.	a	80.	b
9.	b	27.	b	45.	c	63.	b	81.	c
10.	b	28.	a	46.	b	64.	a	82.	c
11.	c	29.	c	47.	b	65.	a	83.	a
12.	c	30.	a	48.	c	66.	b	84.	c
13.	a	31.	b	49.	c	67.	c	85.	c
14.	a	32.	a	50.	a	68.	b	86.	c
15.	c	33.	b	51.	c	69.	b	87.	c
16.	a	34.	c	52.	b	70.	a	88.	c
17.	c	35.	b	53.	c	71.	c	89.	c
18.	c	36.	a	54.	b	72.	b	90.	b

Explanatory Answers

1. **c** The auxiliary *will* must be used in the answer to refer to the auxiliary *will* used in the question.

2. **b** The auxiliary *is* and the pronoun *she* must be used in the answer to refer to the auxiliary *is*, the noun *secretary*, and. the pronoun *she* used in the question.

3. **b** Only "the book" must be mentioned in the answer when the exclusive adverb *instead* is used with "book" in the statement. Remember, *instead* means *in place of*.

4. **b** Because "It doesn't snow very *often* in February," it must be concluded that "we *occasionally* have snow." Remember, *occasionally* means *not often*.

5. **b** Because "the buses *don't start* running at eight o'clock," it must be concluded that "[they] *don't begin* running at eight o'clock." Remember to *start* means to *begin*.

6. **b** Because "John told *Alice* to write the paper," it must be concluded that "*Alice* wrote it." The paper is *for* me, not *by* me.

7. **c** Because the speaker says "[he] decided to study at *Community College*," it must be concluded that he studied there. He gives reasons for *not* studying at State University or City College.

8. **a** Because "I've never heard the orchestra play professionally," it must be concluded that "[they] never played professionally." It is possible that they played professionally and the speaker did not hear them, but that alternative is not one of the choices in the text book.

9. **b** The feminine pronoun *she* must be used in the answer to refer to the feminine name *Mary* used in the question.

10. **b** The adjective phrase *a little* must be used in the answer to refer to the non-count noun *milk* used in the question. Although *some* may be used with either a plural count noun or a non-count noun, choice (c) is not a logical response to the question. Because the speaker says "I *have* some," it is not logical for him to say *yes* in response to the question, "Shall I *buy* some?"

11. **c** "Tom was arrested by the police" is a passive form of the active statement, "The police arrested Tom." Mabel and I were *surprised*, not *arrested*.

12. **c** The frequency number *twice* must be used in the answer when the question phrase *how many times* is used in the question. Remember, the phrase *how many times* means *how often*.

13. **a** The auxiliary *haven't* and the plural pronoun *they* must be used in the answer to refer to the auxiliary *haven't* and the plural noun *officials* used in the question.

14. **a** A choice must be made in the answer between the two possibilities mentioned, "next week" *or* "the week after" when the alternative conjunction *or* is used in the question.

15. **c** Because "Tom called her because we'd received her letter," it must be concluded that "Tom called her . . . because of her letter." The *letter* is the cause.

16. **a** The masculine pronoun *he* must be used in the answer to refer to the masculine name *James* used in the question.

17. **c** Because "Joe wasn't hungry *at all*," it must be concluded that "[he] did*n't* want *anything* to eat." Remember, *not at all* means *not any*.

18. **c** The neuter pronoun *it* must be used in the answer to refer to the neuter noun *check* used in the question.

19. **b** Only the "letter," must be mentioned in the answer when *isn't* is used with "package" in the statement.

20. **a** Because "Bill and Betty left . . . *before* classes were *over* on Friday," it must be concluded that they left *during* classes. Remember, *over* means *finished*.

21. **c** The auxiliary *did* and the pronoun *I* must be used in the answer to refer to the auxiliary *did* and the pronoun *you* used in the question. Remember, *I* or *we* is a correct response to a question with the pronoun *you*.

22. **c** When the question word *where* is used in the question, a place must be mentioned in the answer. Remember, when a statement is followed by a question, the correct answer refers to the question, not the statement.

23. **a** The auxiliary *is* and the neuter pronoun *it* must be used in the answer to refer to the auxiliary *is* and the neuter noun *tea* used in the question.

24. **a** A definite person must be mentioned in the answer when the word *which* is used with *person* in the question. Remember, names or adjective phrases with the definite article *the* are correct responses to questions that require definite answers.

25. **b** The masculine pronoun *he* and the pronoun *me* must be used in the answer to refer to the masculine noun *man* and the pronoun *me* used in the statement.

26. **a** The auxiliary *was* and the pronoun *I* must be used in the answer to refer to the auxiliary *was* and the pronoun *you* used in the question. Remember, *I* or *we* is a correct response to a question with the pronoun *you*. *Was* must be used for agreement between the auxiliary and the pronoun.

27. **b** Because "Ruth *wondered*," it must be concluded that "she *didn't know* when the doctor would come." Remember, to *wonder* means to *be uncertain*.

28. **a** The auxiliary *did* and the neuter pronoun *it* must be used in the answer to refer to the auxiliary *did* and the noun phrase *failing the course* used in the question.

29. **c** Because the speaker says he will "*probably* go see [the game]," it must be concluded that "he *may* go." Remember, *may* means *probably*.

30. **a** The auxiliary *wasn't* and the neuter pronoun *it* must be used in the answer to refer to the auxiliary *wasn't* and the neuter noun *suitcase* used in the question.

31. **b** Because "our neighbors have *never* been friendli*er*," it must be concluded that "[they] are friendli*er* now" *than ever*. Remember, *never more* means *more than ever*.

32. **a** "Jim and his wife are going to be given their certificates [by someone]" is a passive form of the active statement, "Someone will give Jim and his wife their certificates." Because "someone will give them *to them*," it must be concluded that "*they*'ll get them."

33. **b** "The foreign student advisor was helped by the students" is a passive form of the active statement, "The students helped the foreign student advisor."

34. **c** A noun or noun phrase must be used in the answer when the word *what* is used with a form of *be* in the question.

35. **b** Because "she *hadn't begun* to cut the cake when I arrived," it must be concluded that "I arrived *before* the cake had been cut." In both statements, the same chronological order occurs.

36. **a** The auxiliary *is* and the neuter pronoun *it* must be used in the answer to refer to the auxiliary *is* and the neuter pronoun *it* used in the question, "Is it certain?"

37. **a** The auxiliary *do* and the pronoun *they* must be used in the answer to refer to the auxiliary *don't* and the pronoun *they* used in the tag question. Remember, a tag question is a short question at the end of a sentence. Negative tags usually assume an affirmative response.

38. **b** Because "Linda was going to go home *until* winter quarter," it must be concluded that she will *come back* winter quarter. Remember, the preposition *until* means *before*.

39. **b** The auxiliary *is* and the neuter pronoun *it* must be used in the answer to refer to the auxiliary *is* and the neuter place name *Tucson* used in the question. Remember, place names are not masculine or feminine in English.

40. **b** The pronoun *you* and the singular pronoun *it* must be used in the answer to refer to the pronoun *you* and the singular noun *house* used in the statement.

41. **b** The auxiliary *would* must be used in the answer to refer to the auxiliary *would* used in the question.

42. **a**   The auxiliary *do* and the pronoun *they* must be used in the answer to refer to the auxiliary *does* and the collective noun *family* used in the question. Remember, the plural pronoun *they* is a correct response to a question with a collective noun like *family* when the individual members are considered. *Do* must be used for agreement between the auxiliary and the pronoun.

43. **c**   The auxiliary *was* and the subject *it* must be used in the answer to refer to the auxiliary *was* and the pronoun *it* used in the question.

44. **a**   Because "James *asked me*," it must be concluded that "[he] thought that *I knew*."

45. **c**   When the word *when* is used in the question, a time must be mentioned in the answer. Remember, *all of the time* means *always*.

46. **b**   Because "it did*n't stop* raining *until* the afternoon of the wedding," it must be concluded that "it *ended* on the afternoon of the wedding." Remember, the preposition *until* means *before*.

47. **b**   Because "*they told me* where the car was parked," it must be concluded that "*they knew* where it was parked."

48. **c**   The preposition *from* must be used with the name of a specific university in the answer, since *from* is used with the question word *which* in the question.

49. **c**   Because the speaker says "we *ought to* go there to live," it must be concluded that "we *should* live there." Remember, *ought to* means *should*.

50. **a**   The auxiliary *was* and the masculine pronoun *he* must be used in the answer to refer to the auxiliary *was* and the masculine name *James* used in the question.

51. **c**   The preposition *for* must be used with a name in the answer when the preposition *for* is used with the question word *who* in the question.

52. **b**   When the question word *how* is used in the question, directions or an explanation must be mentioned in the answer. The word *by* is implied in the answer "[by] playing baseball."

53. **c**   When the question word *what* is used with *telephone number* in the question, a seven-digit number must be mentioned in the answer. Remember, when a statement is followed by a question, the correct answer refers to the question, not the statement.

54. **b**   An indefinite description must be used in the answer when the question phrase *what kind* is used in the question. Remember, the indefinite articles *an* and *a* are used with adjectives in an indefinite description.

55. **c**   The auxiliary *have* must be used in the answer to refer to the auxiliary *haven't* used in the question.

56. **a**   The auxiliary *has* and the pronoun *it* must be used in the answer to refer to the auxiliary *hasn't* and the pronoun *it* used in the tag question. Remember, a tag question is a short question at the end of a sentence. Negative tags usually assume an affirmative response.

57. **b**   "UCLA was *beaten* by the University of Southern California" is a passive form of the statement, "The University of Southern California [*beat* UCLA]." Remember, to *beat* means to *win a victory over*.

58. **b**   The adjective *some* may be used in the answer to refer to the non-count noun *coffee* used in the question. Although *a little* may be used with a non-count noun, choice (a) is not a logical response to the question. Because the speaker says "I have a little," it is not logical for him to say *yes* in response to the question, "Do you *want* any?"

59. **b** Because "they had a few problems that I *wasn't aware of*," it must be concluded that "I *didn't know* about the problems that they had." Remember, to *not be aware* means to *not know*.

60. **b** The auxiliary *could have* must be used in the answer to refer to the auxiliary *could have* used in the question.

61. **c** Because the speaker says "*a* teacher," it must be concluded that "*one* [teacher] . . . is not from the United States." Remember, the article *a* in English means *one*.

62. **a** The adjective phrase *a few* must be used in the answer to refer to the count noun *cookies* used in the question.

63. **b** When the affirmative adverb *so* is used in the statement, *both* must be mentioned in the answer. Remember, *so* means *also*.

64. **a** The auxiliary *is* must be used with a name in the answer to refer to the auxiliary *is* and the question word *who* used in the question. Remember, *who* refers to people.

65. **a** The neuter pronoun *it* must be used in the answer to refer to the neuter noun *car* used in the question.

66. **b** Because "John *has been sicker* [in the past]," it must be concluded that "[he] *is better* than he was [before]."

67. **c** *Neither* must be mentioned in the answer when *not either* is used in the statement. Remember, *neither* means *not either*.

68. **b** The pronoun *I* must be used in the answer to refer to the pronoun *you* used in the question. Remember, *I* or *we* is a correct response to a question with the pronoun *you*.

69. **b** The auxiliary *is* and the neuter pronoun *it* must be used in the answer to refer to the auxiliary *is* and the neuter noun *food* used in the question.

70. **a** The speaker says, "It's *all right with me*." Remember, to *be all right with someone* means to *be approved of*.

71. **c** Because "Miss Smith doesn't *start* practicing *until* five o'clock," it must be concluded that "she *[begins]* at five o'clock." Remember, the preposition *until* means *before*.

72. **b** When the phrase *how much* is used with the verb *cost* in the question, an amount of money must be mentioned in the answer.

73. **c** Because the speaker says "the seats are *[for the movie that we want to see]*," it must be concluded that the seats are *correct*. Seats for a movie that we did *not* want to see would be *incorrect*.

74. **c** Because the speaker says "we *went*," it must be concluded that "we *attended*" even though we were not invited.

75. **c** A preposition of directional location must be used in the answer when the question word *where* is used with a verb of motion in the question. Remember, *take* is a verb of motion. The prepositions *to*, *down*, *up*, and *across* are directional prepositions.

76. **c** The speaker says he "took a *two-bedroom*." He gives reasons for *not* taking a one-bedroom or an efficiency.

77. **a** Because "Mary told *me* that I should wait," it must be concluded that "*I* waited."

78. **a** The speaker says "*all* of the workbook was used."

79. **c** *Both* "the coffee" and "the water" must be mentioned in the answer since the inclusive adverb *too* is used in the statement. Remember, *too* means *in addition to*.

80. b   The speaker says he "bought *the brown coat*." He gives reasons for *not* buying the red one or the black one.

81. c   The name *Mr. White* and the auxiliary *does* must be used in the answer to refer to the question word *who* and the verb *uses* used in the question. Remember, the auxiliaries *do*, *does*, and *did* are used to refer to all verbs except *be*. *Who* refers to people.

82. c   Because "his wife kept smoking," it must be concluded that "his wife wanted to smoke." Remember, to *keep* means to *continue*.

83. a   Only "London" must be mentioned in the answer since the auxiliary *didn't* is used with "Paris" in the statement.

84. c   "The teacher who recommended you" is a relative clause form of the statement, "the teacher recommended you."

85. c   When the question word *why* is used in the question, an explanation of cause must be given in the answer. Remember, when a statement is followed by a question, the correct answer refers to the question, not the statement.

86. c   *None* must be used in the answer to refer to the negative adjective *no* used in the statement. Remember, *no* means *not one* or *none*.

87. c   Because the speaker says "John's sister didn't help him find an apartment," it must be concluded that "John had to find his apartment [alone]." The speaker says he was *upset*; he does not say he *helped* John.

88. c   "John stopped working" and "his doctor had said that he could continue [working]" are the two clauses in the statement, "John stopped working even though his doctor had said that he could continue."

89. c   Because "Mary told my roommate *she*'d [Mary] study with *me*," it must be concluded that "*Mary* and *I* studied."

90. b   The quantity number *two* must be used in the answer when the question phrase *how many* is used with the noun *friends* in the question. Choice (a) refers to *money*, and choice (c) refers to *time*, not *friends*.

Continued Study
of Aural Comprehension

CHAPTER 3

Continued Study of Aural Comprehension

A THREE-STEP STUDY PROGRAM

Because the Michigan Test of Aural Comprehension is a test of *spoken structures*, you must develop both your knowledge of structures and your skill in listening. Then you must apply your knowledge and skill to the test.

You can do this by following three steps:

1. **Study one or more good grammar textbooks** to improve your knowledge of structures.
2. **Practice listening for specific structures** to improve your skill in listening.
3. **Apply your knowledge and skill to the test.**

Step One: Study One or More Good Grammar Textbooks

There are many good grammar books. Those of you who are enrolled in an English program probably have a good grammar book. *Attend your grammar class every day*. If you do not know the structures already, your class will help you learn them. If you already know the structures, your class will help you practice listening to them. The best preparation for the Michigan Test of Aural Comprehension is daily practice in listening.

If you are not enrolled in an English program, buy a good grammar book or borrow one from the library. There are dozens of good books. Some of the most complete ones are listed:

Bruder, Mary Newton. *Developing Communicative Competence in English as a Second Language*. Pittsburgh, Pennsylvania: University of Pittsburgh Press, 1974.

Danielson, Dorothy, and Hayden, Rebecca. *Using English: Your Second Language*. Englewood Cliffs, New Jersey: Prentice-Hall, 1973.

Frank, Marcella. *Modern English Exercises for Non-Native Speakers: Parts 1, 2, and 3*. Englewood Cliffs, New Jersey: Prentice-Hall, 1972.

Krohn, Robert. *English Sentence Structure*. Ann Arbor, Michigan: University of Michigan Press, 1977.

Praninskas, Jean. *Rapid Review of English Grammar*. Second Edition. Englewood Cliffs, New Jersey: Prentice-Hall, 1975.

Rutherford, William E. *Modern English*. Volumes 1 and 2. New York: Harcourt Brace Jovanovich, 1968.

Step Two: Practice Listening for Specific Structures and Inferences

There are ten specific structures and one inference problem that you should practice listening for. They are listed below, with examples from the Model Tests in this book.

Specific Structures

1. PRONOUNS REFERRING TO NAMES

If a name is masculine, the pronoun that refers to it must be masculine. If a name is feminine, the pronoun that refers to it must be feminine. If a name is a family name, the pronoun that refers to it must be plural. When you hear a name, do you know whether the speaker is referring to a man, a woman, or a family? Can you use the correct pronoun in a short answer?

Examples

"Is *Bob* very busy?"
"Yes, *he* is."

"Are the *Williamses* here yet?"
"Yes, *they* are."

"Did *Philip and Jane* tell you for certain that they were getting a divorce?"
"Yes, *they* did."

"Isn't *Mabel* going to get a phone?"
"No, *she* isn't."

"Was *Betty* at home when you went to see her father?"
"Yes, *she* was."

2. PRONOUNS REFERRING TO NOUNS

If a noun is masculine, the pronoun that refers to it must be masculine. If a noun is feminine, the pronoun that refers to it must be feminine. If a noun is neuter, the pronoun that refers to it must be neuter. When you hear a noun, do you know whether it is masculine, feminine, or neuter? Can you use the correct pronoun in a short answer?

Examples

"Wasn't *the woman's husband* there when she arrived at the airport?"
"No, *he* wasn't."

"Is *next week* when Ruth is taking her vacation?"
"Yes, *it* is."

"Is *the secretary* sure that she sent a copy of the I-20?"
"Yes, *she* is."

"Have *the officials* been sent to the embassy already?"
"No, *they* haven't."

"Is *William's check* here yet?"
"Yes, *it* is."

3. QUANTITY ADJECTIVE PHRASES MODIFYING NOUNS

If the noun is a count noun, the phrase that modifies it must be a count phrase. If the noun is a non-count noun, the phrase that modifies it must be a non-count phrase. When you hear a noun, do you know whether the speaker is using a count or a non-count noun? Can you use the correct quantity adjective phrase in a short answer?

Examples

"Do you have *any homework* tonight?"
"Yes, I have *a little*."

"Do you have *any fresh fish* today?"
"Yes, I still have *some*."

"Shall I buy *some milk*?"
"No, I still have *a little*."

"Do you want *any coffee* while you're studying?"
"No, I have *some*."

"Would you like *some more cookies*?"
"No, thank you. I still have *a few*."

4. AUXILIARY VERBS IN SHORT ANSWERS REFERRING TO AUXILIARY VERBS IN QUESTIONS

If the auxiliary in the question is in the present tense, the auxiliary in the answer must be in the present tense. If the auxiliary in the question is in the past tense, the auxiliary in the answer must be in the past tense. The most common auxiliaries are *be, do, have,* and the modals *will, would, shall, should, may, might, can, could,* and *must*. If the auxiliary in the question is *be,* the auxiliary in the answer must be *be;* if the auxiliary in the question is *do,* the auxiliary in the answer must be *do;* and so on. When you hear a question with an auxiliary, do you know whether the speaker is referring to the present or the past? Can you remember the auxiliary that the speaker used? Can you use the correct auxiliary in a short answer?

Examples

"*Are* the tests graded yet?"
"Yes, they *are*."

"*Is* that woman the best tutor?"
"Yes, she *is*."

"*Does* it take a long time to travel from your country to the United States?"
"Yes, it *does*."

"*Couldn't* you *have* changed your plane reservation if you had wanted to?"
"Yes, I *could have*."

"Mrs. Jones *has* finished typing your report, *hasn't* she?"
"Yes, she *has*."

"*Did* you finally drop the course?"
"Yes, I *did*."

5. MODALS AND SEMI-MODALS

A modal often has the same meaning as a semi-modal. When you hear a modal in a question, can you use the correct semi-modal in a short answer? When you hear a semi-modal in a question, can you use the correct modal in a short answer?

Examples

"This game is supposed to be very good, but I *will not* be able to go see it."
"He *won't* go."

"We're invited, but we *aren't able* to go."
"We *can't* attend."

"Bill won't tell her, but I *will*."
"I'm *going to* tell her."

"We're invited, and we *have to* go."
"We *must* attend."

"The climate is not very good, but we *ought to* go there to live."
"We *should* live there."

6. NEGATIVE PHRASES

A negative phrase or two negative phrases often have the same meaning as an affirmative phrase. When you hear a negative phrase, do you know whether the speaker is referring to a negative or an affirmative? Can you say the sentence or question in another way without changing its meaning?

Examples

"I've *never* heard the orchestra play *more* professionally."
"The orchestra played *more* professionally *than ever*."

"They had *no* problems that I am aware of."
"I *don't* think that they had *any* problems."

"We have *no* teacher who's *not* from the United States."
"*All* of our teachers are from the United States."

"Our neighbors have *never* been friend*lier*."
"Our neighbors are friend*lier now*."

"Bill *isn't* going to graduate this quarter, and his cousin *isn't either*."
"*Neither* Bill *nor* his cousin is graduating."

7. PASSIVE SENTENCES

Passive sentences have the same meaning as active sentences. Passive verbs are used when the speaker wants to emphasize the object of an active sentence. When you hear a passive, can you say the sentence as an active without changing its meaning?

Examples

"Anna's certificate *will be given* to her husband at the ceremony on Friday."
"Someone *will give* Anna's certificate to her husband."
[He'll get it for her.]

"The students *were helped* by the foreign student advisor."
"The foreign student advisor *helped* the students."

"Mabel and I were surprised when Tom *was arrested* by the police."
"The police *arrested* Tom."

"The foreign student advisor *was helped* by the students."
"The students *helped* the foreign student advisor."

"UCLA *was beaten* by the University of Southern California in the last game of the season."
"The University of Southern California *beat* UCLA."
[The University of Southern California won.]

8. CORRELATIVE CONJUNCTIONS

A correlative conjunction is used to include or exclude the information contained in a clause. When you hear a correlative conjunction, do you know whether the speaker is including or excluding? Can you say the sentence or question in another way without changing its meaning?

Examples

"Did you *pass* the course *or fail* it?"
"I *passed* it."

"Bill is going to graduate this quarter, and *so* is his cousin."
"*Both* Bill and his cousin are graduating."

"I'd planned to see the movie, but I read the book *instead*."
"I read *only* the book."

"I asked for a cup of coffee, but the waitress gave me some water *too*."
"I was given *both* coffee and water."

"We were going to stop in London and Paris on the way home, but we *didn't* stop in Paris."
"We stopped *only* in London."

9. TIME RELATIONSHIPS

Verbs and adverbs used in one clause may refer to events before, during, or after events in another clause. When you hear a verb phrase or an adverb, do you know whether the speaker is referring to events before, during, or after events in another clause? Can you say the sentence or question in another way without changing its meaning?

Examples

"The buses *don't stop* running *until* eight o'clock."
"The buses *end* the run *at* eight o'clock."

"Tom called her *before* we received her letter."
"We received her letter *after* Tom had called her."

"It *didn't start* raining *until* the afternoon of the wedding."
"It *began on* the afternoon of the wedding."

"I arrived *just as* she was cutting the cake."
"I arrived *while* the cake was being cut."

"Bill and Betty left for vacation *before* classes were *over* on Friday."
"They left *during* the classes."

10. QUESTION WORDS

The answers to information questions refer to the question words. The most common question words are *who, what, when, where, why, how, how much,* and *how many*. If the question word is *who*, the information in the answer must be a person; if the question word is *what*, the information in the answer must be a noun phrase; and so on. When you hear a question word, do you know what information the speaker wants? Can you answer the question with the correct information?

Examples

"*How many* students are from Saudi Arabia?"
"Only *two* of them."

"*Which* typewriter do you think I should buy?"
"*The* smaller *one*."

"I understand that you're going to transfer, but *when* are you leaving?"
"*Next year*."

"*How many times* did you take the Michigan Test before you scored 80?"
"Only *once*."

"*Who* are you taking the book out *for?*"
"*For Bill*."

"*How much* does the book *cost* for that class?"
"Ten *dollars*."

Inferences

An inference is a conclusion based on facts. When you hear a sentence, do you remember all of the facts it contains? Can you make an inference based on those facts?

Examples

"*Ruth told her doctor* when the baby was due."
"*She knew* when the baby would come."

"*We wondered* where we had parked the car."
"*We didn't know* where it was parked."

"I told *Mary* that she should wait for the taxi driver."
"So *Mary* waited."

"I was upset because *John didn't help his sister* find an apartment."
"*She had to* find her apartment."

"*James asked me* who would win."
"*James thought that I knew* what would happen."

Step Three: Apply Your Knowledge and Skill to the Test

To apply your knowledge and skill means to use information that you have already studied to help you in a new situation.

On the Michigan Test of Aural Comprehension, you won't see and hear exactly the same questions that you have studied in your textbooks. But you will see and hear questions about the specific structures that you have reviewed in Step Two. And the specific structures are explained in your textbooks. If you understand the specific structures in your textbooks, you should understand the questions on your test.

First, memorize the generalizations in your textbooks. Generalizations are often printed in boxes or set apart with a title like *Rule*, *Pattern*, or *Generalization*. The examples, exercises, and drills that often follow are there to help you practice the generalization. *Don't* try to remember all of the examples, exercises, and drills. Just try to remember the generalizations.

A grammar lesson from *Barron's How to Prepare for the TOEFL* is printed on the opposite page. Can you find the generalization? The examples? What should you try to remember?

Now learn to recognize the information from your textbooks as it appears on the test. Sometimes this is difficult because the format in your textbook is not the same as the format on your test. (*Format* means the way information is organized on a page.)

Textbook Format

The exercises below are like the exercises in your textbooks. They are printed in textbook format.

1. Do you need any money?
   Yes, I do. I need a little.

2. Do you need any stamps?
   Yes, I do. I need a few.

3. Would you like cream or sugar in your coffee?
   Yes, I'd like cream, please.

4. Wasn't there a party last night?
   Yes, there was.

5. We should be more careful.
   We ought to be more careful.

6. Bill's girl friend doesn't expect him to call her every week, but he does.
   Bill calls his friend every week.

7. I talked to him while he was on his break.
   I talked to him during his break.

8. John doesn't like waiting, and I don't either.
   John doesn't like waiting, and neither do I.

9. Who did you come with?
   I came with my wife.

10. How much did it cost?
    Six dollars.

Problem 14: Subjunctives

S	V	that	S	verb word	
Mr. Johnson	prefers	that	she	speak	with him personally

Remember that the following verbs are used before *that* and the verb word clause:

ask	prefer
demand	recommend
desire	require
insist	suggest

Avoid using a present or past verb instead of a verb word. Avoid using a modal before the verb word.

noun	that	S	verb word	
The recommendation	that	we	be	evaluated was approved

Remember that the following nouns are used in this pattern:
recommendation
requirement
suggestion

Avoid using a present or past verb instead of a verb word. Avoid using a modal before the verb word.

EXAMPLES:

Incorrect: The doctor suggested that she will not smoke.
Correct: The doctor suggested that she not smoke.

Incorrect: He complied with the requirement that all graduate students in education should write a thesis.
Correct: He complied with the requirement that all graduate students in education write a thesis.

Incorrect: The foreign student advisor recommended that she studied more English before enrolling at the university.
Correct: The foreign student advisor recommended that she study more English before enrolling at the university.

Incorrect: The law requires that everyone has his car checked at least once a year.
Correct: The law requires that everyone have his car checked at least once a year.

Incorrect: She insisted that they should give her a receipt.
Correct: She insisted that they give her a receipt.

Reprinted from *Barron's How to Prepare for the Test of English as a Foreign Language (TOEFL)*

Test Format

The exercises below are the same exercises. But they are printed in test format.

1. Do you need any money?

   a. Yes, just a little, please. ✓
   b. Yes, just a few, please.
   c. No, just a little, please.

2. Do you need any stamps?

   a. Yes, just a little, please.
   b. Yes, just a few, please. ✓
   c. Yes, I have some.

3. Would you like cream or sugar in your coffee?

   a. Yes, I do.
   b. Yes, I have.
   c. Cream, please. ✓

4. Wasn't there a party last night?

   a. Yes, it was.
   b. Yes, there was. ✓
   c. Yes, we were.

5. We ought to be more careful.

   a. We should be more careful. ✓
   b. We may be more careful.
   c. We must be more careful.

6. Bill's friend doesn't expect him to call her every week, but he does.

   a. Bill's friend calls him.
   b. Bill doesn't call his friend.
   c. Bill calls his friend. ✓

7. I talked to him while he was on his break.

   a. I talked to him during his break. ✓
   b. I talked to him before his break.
   c. I talked to him after his break.

8. John doesn't like waiting, and I don't either.

   a. Both John and I like waiting.
   b. John doesn't like waiting, and neither do I. ✓
   c. Only John doesn't like waiting.

9. Who did you come with?

    a. With my wife. ✓

    b. My wife did.

    c. My wife is.

10. How much did it cost?

    a. Six of them.

    b. Only six.

    c. Six dollars. ✓

Can you recognize the information from your textbooks when it is printed in test format? If you can *learn the generalizations* from your textbooks and *recognize the information* when it is printed in test format, you are ready to take the Michigan Test of Aural Comprehension. You can apply your knowledge and skill to the test.

Answer Key

1. a	5. a	8. a
2. b	6. c	9. a
3. c	7. b	10. c
4. b		

OPTIONAL ASSIGNMENTS

Optional means something that you *may* or *may not* do. If you need more practice in listening, you may want to do some of the assignments suggested below. Ask your librarian or language lab assistant for the books and tapes you need.

1. Morley, Joan. *Listening Dictation*. Ann Arbor, Michigan: University of Michigan Press, 1971.

Listen to Part Two of all of the lessons, and answer the multiple choice questions. Part One is not assigned.

2. Kolaitis, Marinna, and Manganari, Efthalia. *The American English Laboratory Workbook*. New York: Rand McNally & Co., 1971.

Listen to the Comprehension Drills for all of the lessons, and answer the multiple choice questions. The Repetition and Substitution Drills are not assigned.

3. Stieglitz, Francine. *Progressive Audiolingual Drills (PALS)*. New York: Regents Publishing Co., Inc., 1970.

Listen to the following exercises:

Unit Four	Drill Number 4	Exercises 1-44
Unit Five	Drill Number 5	Exercises 47-72
Unit Seven	Drill Number 7	Exercises 33-44
Unit Eight	Drill Number 8	Exercises 32-47
Unit Nine	Drill Number 9	Exercises 46-60
Unit Ten	Drill Number 10	Exercises 1-52
Unit Eleven	Drill Number 11	Exercises 1-56
Unit Twelve	Drill Number 12	Exercises 1-59
Unit Fourteen	Drill Number 14	Exercises 16-54
Unit Fifteen	Drill Number 15	Exercises 30-59
Unit Seventeen	Drill Number 17	Exercises 34-55
Unit Eighteen	Drill Number 18	Exercises 28-53
Unit Twenty-Two	Drill Number 22	Exercises 24-35
Unit Twenty-Seven	Drill Number 27	Exercises 31-60
Unit Twenty-Eight	Drill Number 28	Exercises 31-54
Unit Twenty-Nine	Drill Number 29	Exercises 31-54
Unit Thirty	Drill Number 30	Exercises 31-54
Unit Thirty-One	Drill Number 31	Exercises 10-56
Unit Thirty-Two	Drill Number 32	Exercises 44-60
Unit Thirty-Three	Drill Number 33	Exercises 26-59
Unit Thirty-Four	Drill Number 34	Exercises 1-60
Unit Thirty-Six	Drill Number 36	Exercises 1-59

4. Krohn, Robert. *English Sentence Structure*. Ann Arbor, Michigan: University of Michigan Press, 1971.

Listen to the following tapes:

Tape One	Tape Five
Tape Two	Tape Nine
Tape Three	Tape Eleven
Tape Four	

5. Sharpe, Pamela J. *Barron's How to Prepare for the TOEFL (Test of English as a Foreign Language)*. Woodbury, New York: Barron's Educational Series, Inc., 1976.

Listen to Part A of the Listening Comprehension Section of each Model Test, and answer the multiple choice questions. Parts B and C of the Listening Comprehension Section are not assigned.

6. Sharpe, Pamela J. *Barron's Practice Exercises for the TOEFL (Test of English as a Foreign Language)*. Woodbury, New York: Barron's Educational Series, Inc., 1980.

Listen to all of the Exercises in Chapter One, and answer the multiple choice questions.

Practicing Grammar, Vocabulary, and Reading Comprehension

The Michigan Test of English Language Proficiency

CHAPTER 4

The Michigan Test of English Language Proficiency

DESCRIPTION OF THE TEST

The Michigan Test of English Language Proficiency (MTELP) is a test of your ability to answer questions about English grammar, vocabulary, and reading comprehension. It is a multiple-choice test with 100 problems.

There are many forms of the MTELP, each identified by a letter of the alphabet: A, B, C, D, E, F, G, H, M, N, O, P, and so on. All of the forms are at the same level of difficulty.

There are three parts to the test:

Part I—Grammar. Part I tests your ability to use grammatical structures. It contains forty short conversations. Each conversation has a question or statement followed by a response.

Don't try to answer the questions without reading all of the conversation. Understanding the situation is very important in choosing the best answer.

Part II—Vocabulary. Part II tests your ability to use vocabulary. It contains forty sentences of two types—Definition Sentences and Completion Sentences.

Part III—Reading Comprehension. Part III tests your ability to read quickly and to understand what you have read. It contains four reading passages of 100-350 words each. Each passage is followed by five multiple-choice questions.

The passages include readings about history, physical science, social science, and literature, as well as personal anecdotes and general interest passages. The questions include both facts and inferences.

Don't answer the questions based on information that you know or have read in another place. The answers may be different because the information given in the reading passage may be different from what you have learned elsewhere.

Don't stop after each part of the MTELP. Continue working through all three parts. The total time for the test is seventy-five minutes.

Answer Sheet—English Language Proficiency
Model Test One

Name _____ Date _____

Part I—
Grammar

1. a( ) b( ) c( ) d( )	11. a( ) b( ) c( ) d( )	21. a( ) b( ) c( ) d( )	31. a( ) b( ) c( ) d( )
2. a( ) b( ) c( ) d( )	12. a( ) b( ) c( ) d( )	22. a( ) b( ) c( ) d( )	32. a( ) b( ) c( ) d( )
3. a( ) b( ) c( ) d( )	13. a( ) b( ) c( ) d( )	23. a( ) b( ) c( ) d( )	33. a( ) b( ) c( ) d( )
4. a( ) b( ) c( ) d( )	14. a( ) b( ) c( ) d( )	24. a( ) b( ) c( ) d( )	34. a( ) b( ) c( ) d( )
5. a( ) b( ) c( ) d( )	15. a( ) b( ) c( ) d( )	25. a( ) b( ) c( ) d( )	35. a( ) b( ) c( ) d( )
6. a( ) b( ) c( ) d( )	16. a( ) b( ) c( ) d( )	26. a( ) b( ) c( ) d( )	36. a( ) b( ) c( ) d( )
7. a( ) b( ) c( ) d( )	17. a( ) b( ) c( ) d( )	27. a( ) b( ) c( ) d( )	37. a( ) b( ) c( ) d( )
8. a( ) b( ) c( ) d( )	18. a( ) b( ) c( ) d( )	28. a( ) b( ) c( ) d( )	38. a( ) b( ) c( ) d( )
9. a( ) b( ) c( ) d( )	19. a( ) b( ) c( ) d( )	29. a( ) b( ) c( ) d( )	39. a( ) b( ) c( ) d( )
10. a( ) b( ) c( ) d( )	20. a( ) b( ) c( ) d( )	30. a( ) b( ) c( ) d( )	40. a( ) b( ) c( ) d( )

Part II—
Vocabulary

41. a( ) b( ) c( ) d( )	51. a( ) b( ) c( ) d( )	61. a( ) b( ) c( ) d( )	71. a( ) b( ) c( ) d( )
42. a( ) b( ) c( ) d( )	52. a( ) b( ) c( ) d( )	62. a( ) b( ) c( ) d( )	72. a( ) b( ) c( ) d( )
43. a( ) b( ) c( ) d( )	53. a( ) b( ) c( ) d( )	63. a( ) b( ) c( ) d( )	73. a( ) b( ) c( ) d( )
44. a( ) b( ) c( ) d( )	54. a( ) b( ) c( ) d( )	64. a( ) b( ) c( ) d( )	74. a( ) b( ) c( ) d( )
45. a( ) b( ) c( ) d( )	55. a( ) b( ) c( ) d( )	65. a( ) b( ) c( ) d( )	75. a( ) b( ) c( ) d( )
46. a( ) b( ) c( ) d( )	56. a( ) b( ) c( ) d( )	66. a( ) b( ) c( ) d( )	76. a( ) b( ) c( ) d( )
47. a( ) b( ) c( ) d( )	57. a( ) b( ) c( ) d( )	67. a( ) b( ) c( ) d( )	77. a( ) b( ) c( ) d( )
48. a( ) b( ) c( ) d( )	58. a( ) b( ) c( ) d( )	68. a( ) b( ) c( ) d( )	78. a( ) b( ) c( ) d( )
49. a( ) b( ) c( ) d( )	59. a( ) b( ) c( ) d( )	69. a( ) b( ) c( ) d( )	79. a( ) b( ) c( ) d( )
50. a( ) b( ) c( ) d( )	60. a( ) b( ) c( ) d( )	70. a( ) b( ) c( ) d( )	80. a( ) b( ) c( ) d( )

(Continued on next page)

Part III—
Reading Comprehension

81. a( )   85. a( )   89. a( )   93. a( )   97. a( )
    b( )   b( )   b( )   b( )   b( )
    c( )   c( )   c( )   c( )   c( )
    d( )   d( )   d( )   d( )   d( )

82. a( )   86. a( )   90. a( )   94. a( )   98. a( )
    b( )   b( )   b( )   b( )   b( )
    c( )   c( )   c( )   c( )   c( )
    d( )   d( )   d( )   d( )   d( )

83. a( )   87. a( )   91. a( )   95. a( )   99. a( )
    b( )   b( )   b( )   b( )   b( )
    c( )   c( )   c( )   c( )   c( )
    d( )   d( )   d( )   d( )   d( )

84. a( )   88. a( )   92. a( )   96. a( )   100. a( )
    b( )   b( )   b( )   b( )   b( )
    c( )   c( )   c( )   c( )   c( )
    d( )   d( )   d( )   d( )   d( )

MODEL TEST ONE
ENGLISH LANGUAGE PROFICIENCY

100 Questions

75 Minutes

Part I—Grammar

Directions

There are forty problems in this part, with four possible answers for each problem. Each problem is part of a conversation. In each conversation, a word or a phrase is missing. Following the conversation are four possible answers that might be used to complete the conversation. After you read each conversation, read the four possible answers, (a), (b), (c), and (d). Choose the one that would be best used to complete the conversation.

Don't stop after you finish this part. Continue to Part II.

SAMPLE TEST ITEMS

You will read:

1. "Have a good trip Mr. Brown."
   "Thank you. _____ anyone need to reach me, I will be staying at the Hyatt Regency."

   a. Does
   b. Can
   c. Had
   d. Should

2. "Does anyone else know about this?"
   "Nobody _____ my sister."

   a. like
   b. although
   c. but
   d. until

3. "Do you play tennis?"
   "Not any more, but we _____."

   a. used to
   b. used to do
   c. used to did
   d. used to was

4. "I hear that this is your anniversary."
   "It is. By this time next year, we _____ for fifty years."

   a. will be married
   b. will married
   c. will have been married
   d. will have married

You should mark:

1.		2.		3.		4.	
a ( )		a ( )		a (x)		a ( )	
b ( )		b ( )		b ( )		b ( )	
c ( )		c (x)		c ( )		c (x)	
d (x)		d ( )		d ( )		d ( )	

Model Test—Grammar

1. "What are you looking for?"
   "I can't remember where I _____ my glasses."

   a. leave
   b. left
   c. had left
   d. was left

2. "Didn't you forget to count your living expenses when you wrote up this budget?"
   "No. That _____ into consideration."

   a. has taken
   b. has been taken
   c. is been taken
   d. is been taking

3. "My paper isn't finished."
   "Why don't you tell him that you need a _____ time?"

   a. few more
   b. some more
   c. little more
   d. small more

4. "Why do you look so sad?"
   "My sister wanted _____ to her wedding, but I couldn't."

   a. I go
   b. me to go
   c. me going
   d. that I go

5. "What's this button for?"
   "It _____ the tape."

   a. start
   b. is start
   c. is to start
   d. is for to start

6. "Has my son caused you any problems?"
   "Not at all. He has been very _____."

   a. cooperation
   b. cooperative
   c. cooperating
   d. cooperated

7. "I don't like your attitude."
   "I don't care _____."

   a. if or not you like it
   b. whether you like it or not
   c. do you like it or not
   d. you like it or not

8. "Why are you standing out here in the hall?"
   "The nurse asked us if we wouldn't please _____ outside while the doctor gave Bill his examination."

   a. waiting
   b. wait
   c. waited
   d. to wait

9. "What did he do?"
   "He ran a red light; _____, when the police officer stopped him, he refused to take the sobriety test."

   a. otherwise
   b. moreover
   c. although
   d. therefore

10. "Do you know Mr. Brown?"
    "Yes. There's no one more generous _____ he is."

    a. than
    b. like
    c. to
    d. as

11. "I always get confused about tipping in this country."
    "Usually you _____ to leave 15 percent for a waiter or waitress. Taxi drivers expect 10 or 15 percent, too."

    a. ought
    b. should
    c. might
    d. can

12. "Did you get my letter?"
"Yes, I _____ received it."

   a. has
   b. was
   c. is
   d. have

13. "What did your parents think about your decision?"
"They always let me _____ what I think I should."

   a. to do
   b. do
   c. doing
   d. did

14. "What do you do when you get a headache?"
"Since I'm allergic to aspirin, I take Tylenol _____."

   a. instead of
   b. rather than
   c. instead
   d. rather

15. "Are you going to take the job Mr. Smith offered you?"
"I don't know yet, but it's worth _____ about, isn't it?"

   a. to think
   b. to be thinking
   c. to be thought
   d. thinking

16. "What happened?"
"We _____ for an hour when the bus finally came."

   a. waited
   b. have waited
   c. have been waiting
   d. had been waiting

17. "Where's Nancy?"
"I don't know. _____ forgotten the appointment?"

   a. She might
   b. Have she might
   c. Might have she
   d. Might she have

18. "Are you afraid to drive home?"
"Yes. I wish _____ stop snowing."

   a. would
   b. it
   c. it would
   d. it will

19. "Did you have to go to court?"
"No, I didn't, but I would _____ if my lawyer hadn't been so good."

   a. had
   b. have
   c. be
   d. do

20. "Why are you staring?"
"I've never seen _____ tree before."

   a. that kind
   b. that kind of
   c. such kind
   d. such

21. "Do you need my husband's signature?"
"No. _____ you or Mr. Jones can sign this."

   a. Either
   b. Also
   c. Both
   d. That

22. "Why didn't Susan join the International Students Organization?"
"She objected to _____ dues."

   a. we charge
   b. us charge
   c. us charging
   d. our charging

23. "What can I get my friend for her birthday?"
"That depends on how much _____ to spend."

   a. do you want
   b. you want
   c. you do want
   d. want you

24. "What do you want to do?"
"Let's try to convince everyone to agree tonight; _____ we'll have to have another meeting."

   a. anyway
   b. otherwise
   c. although
   d. moreover

25. "Are you going to go with us on the tour?"
"I'd like to, but with my exams on Monday, I know I really _____."

   a. wouldn't
   b. couldn't
   c. shouldn't
   d. hadn't

26. "How was the movie?"
"To tell the truth, it was rather _____."

   a. disappointing
   b. disappointment
   c. disappoint
   d. disappointed

27. "My watch started up again."
"You should take it to be repaired _____ it's working now."

   a. even though
   b. in spite of
   c. despite
   d. however

28. "Do the Smiths live next door to you?"
"No, but they _____."

   a. used to
   b. used to do
   c. used to was
   d. used to did

29. "Jeff is so lonely."
"I'd like him _____ a nice girl."

   a. finds
   b. to find
   c. finding
   d. find

30. "What happened in physics class today?"
"Nothing much. Dr. Johnson spent most of the hour _____ the book."

   a. referring
   b. referring to
   c. referring of
   d. referring from

31. "I was so sorry to hear about Jack."
"If he had made more friends here, he might _____."

   a. have stayed
   b. have stay
   c. stays
   d. stay

32. "I'd like to go, but I have a date on Saturday."
"That's okay. If we leave today, we can probably be back _____ the weekend."

   a. at
   b. by
   c. to
   d. in

33. "Do you want to go by the lake on the way back?"
"Let's see how much gas _____ is in the tank before we decide."

   a. it
   b. they
   c. there
   d. their

34. "How many _____ do you have?"
"I have six boys and one girl."

   a. childs
   b. child
   c. children
   d. childrens

35. "Was Barbara upset about the misunderstanding?"
"Yes, she was _____ upset that she cried about it afterwards."

   a. very
   b. so
   c. such
   d. too

36. "I couldn't talk to Mrs. Khandari very well, because my Arabic isn't very good yet."
"_____ there, he would have been able to interpret for you."

   a. Had John been
   b. John had been
   c. John was
   d. Was John

37. "I wish you would just forget about it."
"I can't. I want to know _____ she said about us."

   a. that
   b. which
   c. what
   d. it

38. "How is your meal?"
"Good, thank you. The salad tastes especially _____ today."

   a. fresh
   b. freshly
   c. freshness
   d. freshing

39. "Will you be able to go swimming with us?"
"I'll try, but I'm not sure that I _____."

   a. may
   b. can
   c. can to
   d. go to

40. "Whose luggage is this?"
"I believe it's _____."

   a. him
   b. his
   c. he's
   d. he

Part II—Vocabulary

Directions

There are forty problems in this part, with four possible answers for each problem. The problems consist of sentences of two types. In Definition Sentences, a word or phrase is underlined. After you read the sentence, read the four possible answers, (a), (b), (c), and (d). Choose the one that is the best definition of the underlined word or phrase. In Completion Sentences, a word or phrase is missing. After you read the sentence, read the four possible answers, (a), (b), (c), and (d). Choose the one that would best complete the sentence.

Don't stop after you finish this part. Continue to Part III.

SAMPLE TEST ITEMS:

Definition Sentences

You will read:
1. My favorite color is <u>crimson</u>.

    a. green
    b. blue
    c. red
    d. yellow

2. He had a broad <u>smile</u> on his face when he opened his present.

    a. grin
    b. chin
    c. groan
    d. frown

You should mark:

1. a ( )   2. a (x)
   b ( )   b ( )
   c (x)   c ( )
   d ( )   d ( )

Completion Sentences

You will read:
3. The basement was very dark and _____.

    a. dump
    b. plump
    c. limp
    d. damp

4. Twenty-six _____ have been added to the Constitution since it was written in 1787.

    a. commandments
    b. amendments
    c. acknowledgments
    d. measurements

You should mark:

3. a ( )   4. a ( )
   b ( )   b (x)
   c ( )   c ( )
   d (x)   d ( )

Model Test—Vocabulary

41. The National Safety Council urges drivers and passengers to wear seat belts as a _____ against injury.

    a. precaution
    b. convention
    c. destruction
    d. frustration

42. He was very upset when he received <u>a negative reply</u> to his request to transfer to another school.

    a. dismissal
    b. removal
    c. approval
    d. refusal

43. Because there is great <u>variation</u> in the quality of diamonds, stones of the same size may not cost the same price.

    a. difference
    b. similarity
    c. disagreement
    d. agreement

44. It is written in a proverb that <u>honorable</u> women are to be prized more highly than rubies.

    a. tedious
    b. conspicuous
    c. virtuous
    d. illustrious

45. At special schools for animals, dogs are taught to be _____.

    a. obedient
    b. obligated
    c. obstinate
    d. obsolete

46. When the king died, his son was named as his _____.

    a. suffix
    b. supplement
    c. successor
    d. sequel

47. There are several hundred clubs on campus to give students with <u>similar</u> interests an opportunity to get to know each other.

    a. mutual
    b. unusual
    c. dual
    d. cordial

48. If the lawyer can prove that the man was <u>rational</u> when he committed the murder, the judge can order the death sentence.

    a. vain
    b. tame
    c. lame
    d. sane

49. Some cold medications can <u>quicken</u> the heart rate.

    a. start
    b. increase
    c. decrease
    d. stop

50. Fiction books are on the _____ by the card catalog.

    a. crates
    b. trunks
    c. shelves
    d. baskets

51. According to the Bible, the Talmud, and the Koran, the first people were prohibited by God to eat a certain fruit in the Garden of Eden.

    a. flattered
    b. encouraged
    c. forbidden
    d. escorted

52. The music for the 1980 Olympic Games was composed by Chuck Mangione, a gifted musician who plays piano, organ, flute, _____, and many other instruments.

    a. trumpet
    b. quartet
    c. skillet
    d. cabinet

53. The <u>examples</u> for the experiment should be kept in a cool, dark place.

    a. spectators
    b. species
    c. spectrum
    d. specimens

54. The guerrilla army tried to _____ the government.

    a. overcharge
    b. overdo
    c. overlook
    d. overthrow

55. In the children's game called "hide and seek," the children must try to _____ back to a certain place without being seen.

    a. sneak
    b. chaste
    c. rash
    d. joke

56. The Republican Party <u>nominated</u> Ronald Reagan to run for President in 1980.

    a. considered
    b. named
    c. refused
    d. discussed

57. Many psychologists agree that it is not good to <u>suppress</u> anger.
    a. hide
    b. show
    c. cause
    d. believe

58. _____ is equal to sixteen ounces.
    a. A degree
    b. An acre
    c. A ton
    d. A pint

59. The social security system provides _____ for retired citizens.
    a. wages
    b. pensions
    c. profits
    d. rewards

60. Thousands of spectators <u>crowded</u> into the stadium in order to see the football game.
    a. wandered
    b. jammed
    c. dispersed
    d. skipped

61. In the Midwest, most fruit <u>matures</u> in June, July, and August.
    a. ripens
    b. blooms
    c. withers
    d. harvests

62. The _____ of Panama is a narrow strip of land connecting North and South America.
    a. peninsula
    b. isthmus
    c. island
    d. continent

63. Since there is no doorbell, just _____ on the door.
    a. slap
    b. rap
    c. clap
    d. pat

64. Almost everyone on the U.S. amateur boxing team was killed in a very <u>tragic</u> plane crash.
    a. sudden
    b. unfortunate
    c. famous
    d. strange

65. Many trees and _____ were planted throughout the United States during Lyndon Johnson's term as President, because his wife encouraged it.
    a. shrugs
    b. shades
    c. shrubs
    d. shrines

66. The driver entered a(n) _____ of "not guilty" to the charge of operating a car without a proper license.
    a. solution
    b. receipt
    c. echo
    d. plea

67. The Thanksgiving turkey is usually stuffed with bread <u>pieces</u> and herbs.
    a. peelings
    b. remnants
    c. crumbs
    d. grounds

68. For each _____ living in your home, you may deduct one thousand dollars from your taxable income.
    a. subject
    b. dependent
    c. captive
    d. executive

69. There are many different kinds of snakes in the _____ house at the zoo.
    a. servant
    b. serpent
    c. vigor
    d. vapor

70. In spite of everything that has happened, she has a very serene expression on her face.

    a. angry
    b. frightened
    c. calm
    d. happy

71. When you converse with people whom you don't know well, it is always correct to comment about the weather.

    a. meet
    b. talk
    c. do business
    d. travel

72. _____ in the affairs of state by another power will be considered an act of war.

    a. Interference
    b. Contribution
    c. Document
    d. Objectives

73. Although most young couples believe that theirs will be a _____ relationship, 50 percent of all marriages result in divorce.

    a. trying
    b. startling
    c. lasting
    d. shocking

74. Conditions in some prisons today are not much better than those in the prisons of former times.

    a. dungeons
    b. castles
    c. hamlets
    d. monarchs

75. Christian Dior is famous for beautiful perfumes.

    a. flavors
    b. fragrances
    c. noises
    d. images

76. The plans for _____ of the shopping center include the construction of six additional buildings and a parking area.

    a. excursion
    b. explosion
    c. extinction
    d. expansion

77. When she fainted, her friends opened a window and put cold water on her face to _____ her.

    a. revive
    b. refine
    c. revise
    d. reverse

78. If you already have a modular jack in the wall of your apartment, you can put in your own telephone.

    a. insure
    b. install
    c. instill
    d. inspect

79. We knew by the _____ look on her face that the letter had brought bad news.

    a. stubborn
    b. stricken
    c. strict
    d. sturdy

80. Disney World is a gigantic amusement park in Orlando, Florida.

    a. large
    b. expensive
    c. beautiful
    d. new

Part III—Reading Comprehension

Directions

In this part, there are four reading passages with five problems for each passage. In order to answer the problems, you must be able to read for facts and for inferences; that is, you must be able to understand information that is stated and information that is implied.

The problems are of two types. In the first type, Questions, a question is given. After you read the passage and the question, read the four possible answers, (a), (b), (c), and (d). Choose the one that is the best answer to the question. In the second type, Completions, an incomplete sentence is given. After you read the passage and the incomplete sentence, read the four possible answers, (a), (b), (c), and (d). Choose the one that would best complete the sentence.

Don't spend too much time on one passage, or you may not have time to finish the test.

SAMPLE TEST PASSAGE: FACTS

You will read:

About two-thirds of Ohio's twenty-six million acres is rich farmland. Although Ohio is ranked thirty-fifth among the states in area, it ranks eleventh in the amount of land cultivated and in cash receipts from the sale of farm products. It ranks first in the production of winter wheat. Farming provides jobs for nearly one-fifth of the people in the state and food exports for people in other states and other nations.

1. How does Ohio rank among the states in the amount of farm products cultivated?

   a. first
   b. eleventh
   c. twenty-sixth
   d. thirty-fifth

2. According to this paggage, farming in Ohio provides jobs for

   a. other states and nations
   b. other states
   c. other nations
   d. Ohio

You should mark:

1. a ( ) 2. a ( )
    b (x)   b ( )
    c ( )   c ( )
    d ( )   d (x)

SAMPLE TEST PASSAGE: INFERENCE

You will read:

That night, when the court reconvened, George Graham Vest addressed the jury. In his final argument, he stated that he was not interested in the evidence previously presented, nor was he interested in the legalities surrounding a $150 property loss. What concerned him was that a man's pet and friend had been killed. As he spoke, he recalled other dogs that had comforted their masters throughout history. By the time he began to talk about Old Drum, the jury was in tears.

3. Who was George Graham Vest?

    a. a doctor
    b. a lawyer
    c. a musician
    d. a minister

4. From this passage, we may conclude that

    a. a dog killed a man
    b. a man killed a dog
    c. a dog got lost
    d. a man got lost

You should mark:

3. a ( )   4. a ( )
    b (x)   b (x)
    c ( )   c ( )
    d ( )   d ( )

Model Test—Reading Comprehension

For several years, scientists have been testing a substance called interferon, a potential wonder drug that is proving to be effective in treating a variety of ailments, including virus infections, bacteria infections, and tumors. To date, the new drug has provoked no negative reaction of sufficient significance to discourage its use. But in spite of its success, last year only one gram was produced in the entire world.

The reason for the scarcity lies in the structure of interferon. A species specific protein, the interferon produced from one animal species cannot be used in treating another animal species. In other words, to treat human beings, only interferon produced by human beings may be used. The drug is produced by infecting white blood cells with a virus. Fortunately, it is so potent that the amount given each patient per injection is very small.

Unlike antibiotics, interferon does not attack germs directly. Instead, it makes unaffected cells resistant to infection, and prevents the multiplication of viruses within cells.

As you might conclude, one of the most dramatic uses of interferon has been in the treatment of cancer. Dr. Hans Strander, research physician at Sweden's famous Karolinska Institute, has treated more than one hundred cancer patients with the new drug. Among a group of selected patients who had undergone surgical procedures for advanced cancer, half were given conventional treatments and the other half were given interferon. The survival rate over a three-year period was 70 percent among those who were treated with interferon as compared with only 10 to 30 percent among those who had received the conventional treatments.

In the United States, a large-scale project supported by the American Cancer Society is now underway. If the experiment is successful, interferon could become one of the greatest medical discoveries of our time.

81. What is the difference between antibiotics and interferon?

    a. Interferon has serious side effects, whereas antibiotics do not.
    b. Interferon is available in large supply, whereas antibiotics are not.
    c. Antibiotics are very potent, while interferon is not.
    d. Antibiotics kill germs by attacking them directly, while interferon does not.

82. What effect does interferon have on infection?

    a. It provokes a negative reaction.
    b. It keeps healthy cells from becoming infected.
    c. It causes healthy cells to grow.
    d. It attacks viruses.

83. Interferon is produced by

    a. infecting viruses, bacteria, and tumors with a drug
    b. infecting proteins with a virus
    c. infecting white blood cells with a virus
    d. infecting viruses with proteins

84. Interferon has not been more widely used because it is

    a. still very dangerous
    b. not yet available in the United States
    c. difficult to produce in large quantities
    d. not effective in human beings

85. What were the results of Dr. Strander's experiments with interferon?

    a. Half of the patients who received interferon reacted favorably.
    b. At the end of three years, all of the patients who had not received interferon had died.
    c. Most of the patients who received interferon also needed conventional treatments.
    d. Most of the patients who received interferon were still alive after three years.

In Henry Wadsworth Longfellow's fanciful poem entied "Paul Revere's Ride," complete credit was given to Paul Revere for alerting the American colonists to the coming of the British troops and thereby for sparking the Revolutionary War at Lexington. Although an utter corruption of truth, the myth has persisted to the present day because of the popularity of the poem.

Actually, on that fateful day in April of 1775, Commander Joseph Warren sent two young men out on horseback to alert the American Rebels between Boston and Lexington that the British were coming. One was indeed Paul Revere, and the other was William Dawes. In fact, it was Dawes who rode first, rode longer, and performed the task better. Revere got sidetracked and was finally captured by the British near the end of his ride.

86. According to this passage, who should receive the most credit for alerting the colonists that the British were coming?

    a. Henry Wadsworth Longfellow
    b. Paul Revere
    c. Joseph Warren
    d. William Dawes

87. The author mentions the year 1775 because

    a. it was the date that Longfellow's poem appeared
    b. the British and the Americans were engaged in war on that date
    c. it was the date that the war between the British and the Americans ended
    d. it was the date that Boston and Lexington were established

88. Paul Revere is remembered because

    a. he was captured by the British
    b. he rode with William Dawes
    c. Longfellow wrote a poem about him
    d. Commander Warren promoted him

89. Where did the Revolutionary War begin?

    a. in Britain
    b. in Lexington
    c. in Rebels
    d. in Boston

90. From your reading of this passage, which of the following statements is true?

    a. Although Paul Revere did not ride as far as William Dawes, he avoided being captured.
    b. William Dawes rode first, but Paul Revere did a better job.
    c. William Dawes got lost near the end of his ride.
    d. Paul Revere's ride was generally inferior to that of William Dawes.

The purpose of this book is to provide you with practice in spelling English. It is not a book that treats the complex rules of English orthography. Neither does it teach you how to use a dictionary. Its main objective is to introduce regular spelling patterns; that is, to present a regular system for spelling a large group of words. By learning these patterns, and by practicing them, you will master thousands of words.

Of course, there are exceptions to spelling patterns, which must be learned one word at a time. But, unlike some educators, I do not believe that learning to spell English is an impossible task, in spite of the exceptions. And I believe that this book of patterns will help you.

91. The author believes that

    a. it is not possible to learn the exceptions to spelling patterns
    b. there are no exceptions to the spelling patterns in his book
    c. exceptions to spelling patterns must be learned one word at a time
    d. exceptions to spelling patterns must always be looked up in a dictionary

92. In the author's opinion, the best way to learn how to spell is to learn

    a. all of the words one at a time
    b. patterns that are correct for a large number of words
    c. how to use a dictionary
    d. the complex rules of English orthography

93. The main purpose of the book is to

    a. present all of the rules of English spelling
    b. list the exceptions to regular spelling patterns
    c. teach students to use the dictionary
    d. provide practice in using regular spelling patterns

94. After using the book, a student should be able to

    a. spell all of the words in the English language
    b. spell thousands of English words correctly
    c. spell all of the exceptions to the rules of English orthography
    d. spell all of the words in an English dictionary

95. In the author's opinion, other educators

    a. agree with him when he says that English spelling can be learned
    b. agree with him when he says that English spelling cannot be learned
    c. disagree with him when he says that English spelling can be learned
    d. disagree with him when he says that English spelling cannot be learned

On Christmas Eve, 1492, Columbus's flagship, the *Santa Maria,* ran aground on a coral reef off the coast of Haiti. Since then, many attempts have been made to find and recover the ship.

Between 1967 and 1972, Fred Dickson made four explorations of the coral reef in Cap Haitien Bay where Edwin Link had found an anchor that he believed might belong to the flagship. During the first excavation of the coral mound, Dickson and his crew found a layer of ballast stone about two feet below the surface. At the twelve-foot level, they found numerous pieces of wood, copper and brass bolts, iron rods, and a few silver nails, presumably from a piece of armor. Probably the most significant find was some pottery that had been buried between 1375 and 1575.

In later excavations, Dickson's crew continued hacking away at the coral and mud, digging a trench four or five feet wide and eighteen inches deep. But they found nothing that would either prove or disprove the possibility that the *Santa Maria* was buried there.

In 1972, using sophisticated electronic equipment, Dickson discovered an object about seventy-five feet southeast of the coral reef that he had been exploring. It was about one hundred feet long. That it was a ship was certain. Whether it was the *Santa Maria* is still an open question.

96. Who was Edwin Link?

    a. the archaeologist who made four explorations of Cap Haitien Bay
    b. the explorer who found an anchor that may have belonged to the *Santa Maria*
    c. a member of Fred Dickson's crew
    d. the diver who discovered a sunken ship in Cap Haitien Bay

97. What was the most important find during Dickson's first excavation?

   a. a ship
   b. some ballast stone
   c. an anchor
   d. some pottery

98. The silver nails were probably from

   a. the ship's flagstaff
   b. a suit of armor
   c. some sophisticated electronic equipment
   d. a wooden box

99. Where was the buried ship discovered?

   a. in the excavation trench
   b. one hundred feet from the coral reef
   c. seventy-five feet from the coral reef
   d. under the coral mound

100. The object that Dickson found in 1972

   a. was the *Santa Maria*
   b. was not the *Santa Maria*
   c. may be the *Santa Maria*
   d. was not a ship

Answer Sheet—English Language Proficiency Model Test Two

Name_____ Date_____

Part I—
Grammar

1. a( ) b( ) c( ) d( )	11. a( ) b( ) c( ) d( )	21. a( ) b( ) c( ) d( )	31. a( ) b( ) c( ) d( )
2. a( ) b( ) c( ) d( )	12. a( ) b( ) c( ) d( )	22. a( ) b( ) c( ) d( )	32. a( ) b( ) c( ) d( )
3. a( ) b( ) c( ) d( )	13. a( ) b( ) c( ) d( )	23. a( ) b( ) c( ) d( )	33. a( ) b( ) c( ) d( )
4. a( ) b( ) c( ) d( )	14. a( ) b( ) c( ) d( )	24. a( ) b( ) c( ) d( )	34. a( ) b( ) c( ) d( )
5. a( ) b( ) c( ) d( )	15. a( ) b( ) c( ) d( )	25. a( ) b( ) c( ) d( )	35. a( ) b( ) c( ) d( )
6. a( ) b( ) c( ) d( )	16. a( ) b( ) c( ) d( )	26. a( ) b( ) c( ) d( )	36. a( ) b( ) c( ) d( )
7. a( ) b( ) c( ) d( )	17. a( ) b( ) c( ) d( )	27. a( ) b( ) c( ) d( )	37. a( ) b( ) c( ) d( )
8. a( ) b( ) c( ) d( )	18. a( ) b( ) c( ) d( )	28. a( ) b( ) c( ) d( )	38. a( ) b( ) c( ) d( )
9. a( ) b( ) c( ) d( )	19. a( ) b( ) c( ) d( )	29. a( ) b( ) c( ) d( )	39. a( ) b( ) c( ) d( )
10. a( ) b( ) c( ) d( )	20. a( ) b( ) c( ) d( )	30. a( ) b( ) c( ) d( )	40. a( ) b( ) c( ) d( )

Part II—
Vocabulary

41. a( ) b( ) c( ) d( )	51. a( ) b( ) c( ) d( )	61. a( ) b( ) c( ) d( )	71. a( ) b( ) c( ) d( )
42. a( ) b( ) c( ) d( )	52. a( ) b( ) c( ) d( )	62. a( ) b( ) c( ) d( )	72. a( ) b( ) c( ) d( )
43. a( ) b( ) c( ) d( )	53. a( ) b( ) c( ) d( )	63. a( ) b( ) c( ) d( )	73. a( ) b( ) c( ) d( )
44. a( ) b( ) c( ) d( )	54. a( ) b( ) c( ) d( )	64. a( ) b( ) c( ) d( )	74. a( ) b( ) c( ) d( )
45. a( ) b( ) c( ) d( )	55. a( ) b( ) c( ) d( )	65. a( ) b( ) c( ) d( )	75. a( ) b( ) c( ) d( )
46. a( ) b( ) c( ) d( )	56. a( ) b( ) c( ) d( )	66. a( ) b( ) c( ) d( )	76. a( ) b( ) c( ) d( )
47. a( ) b( ) c( ) d( )	57. a( ) b( ) c( ) d( )	67. a( ) b( ) c( ) d( )	77. a( ) b( ) c( ) d( )
48. a( ) b( ) c( ) d( )	58. a( ) b( ) c( ) d( )	68. a( ) b( ) c( ) d( )	78. a( ) b( ) c( ) d( )
49. a( ) b( ) c( ) d( )	59. a( ) b( ) c( ) d( )	69. a( ) b( ) c( ) d( )	79. a( ) b( ) c( ) d( )
50. a( ) b( ) c( ) d( )	60. a( ) b( ) c( ) d( )	70. a( ) b( ) c( ) d( )	80. a( ) b( ) c( ) d( )

(Continued on next page)

Part III—
Reading Comprehension

81.	a( ) b( ) c( ) d( )	**85.**	a( ) b( ) c( ) d( )	**89.**	a( ) b( ) c( ) d( )	**93.**	a( ) b( ) c( ) d( )	**97.**	a( ) b( ) c( ) d( )
82.	a( ) b( ) c( ) d( )	**86.**	a( ) b( ) c( ) d( )	**90.**	a( ) b( ) c( ) d( )	**94.**	a( ) b( ) c( ) d( )	**98.**	a( ) b( ) c( ) d( )
83.	a( ) b( ) c( ) d( )	**87.**	a( ) b( ) c( ) d( )	**91.**	a( ) b( ) c( ) d( )	**95.**	a( ) b( ) c( ) d( )	**99.**	a( ) b( ) c( ) d( )
84.	a( ) b( ) c( ) d( )	**88.**	a( ) b( ) c( ) d( )	**92.**	a( ) b( ) c( ) d( )	**96.**	a( ) b( ) c( ) d( )	**100.**	a( ) b( ) c( ) d( )

MODEL TEST TWO
ENGLISH LANGUAGE PROFICIENCY

100 Questions

75 Minutes

Part I—Grammar

Directions

There are forty problems in this part, with four possible answers for each problem. Each problem is part of a conversation. In each conversation, a word or a phrase is missing. Following the conversation are four possible answers that might be used to complete the conversation. After you read each conversation, read the four possible answers, (a), (b), (c), and (d). Choose the one that would be best used to complete the conversation.

Don't stop after you finish this part. Continue to Part II.

---

1. "Is this the house that you told me about?"
   "Yes, _____."

   a. that's
   b. that's the one
   c. that's the it
   d. that's this

2. "Why don't you charge it?"
   "The bank didn't give _____ a credit card, because I haven't been in the country long enough."

   a. me
   b. my
   c. to me
   d. for me

3. "I didn't know that Carol was a waitress here."
   "She _____ here on Saturdays since June."

   a. has been working
   b. has working
   c. having working
   d. has been worked

4. "The Johnsons looked concerned."
   "Could they _____ worried about their son?"

   a. has been
   b. been
   c. have been
   d. being

5. "Did you check your paper?"
   "No, I _____ it now."

   a. checking
   b. am checking
   c. check
   d. checked

6. "Are you going to the fair?"
   "Yes. You're welcome to go with us, so long _____ you don't have to come back right away."

   a. that
   b. to
   c. as
   d. so

7. "I'm trying to remember their phone number."
"Why don't you _____ in the phone book?"

    a.   look it up
    b.   look up it
    c.   look up
    d.   look it

8. "His grandmother still treats him like a child."
"She can't imagine _____ grown up."

    a.   he
    b.   him
    c.   his
    d.   he'll

9. "What's your hobby?"
"I like _____ of sports."

    a.   any kinds
    b.   kinds
    c.   all kind
    d.   all kinds

10. "Did you know that she was expecting a baby?"
"No. We _____ to get the news."

    a.   were surprise
    b.   were surprising
    c.   were surprised
    d.   surprised

11. "Mary said that you locked your keys in your car last night and had to walk home."
"Never _____!"

    a.   I have been so embarrassed
    b.   have I been so embarrassed
    c.   have been I so embarrassed
    d.   I have so embarrassed been

12. "Can't you take a few days off from work to go with me to New York?"
"Sure. _____ my way and I'll be glad to go."

    a.   Pay
    b.   If you pay
    c.   That you pay
    d.   Paying

13. "Did you like the book that I gave you?"
"_____ the novels that I've read, I enjoyed this one the most."

    a.   Of all
    b.   All of
    c.   For all
    d.   From all

14. "What would you like for dinner?"
"_____ we're both so tired, why don't we order a pizza?"

    a.   However
    b.   Moreover
    c.   Since
    d.   Although

15. "Did you enjoy your guests?"
"Yes. Their children are so well _____ that I always enjoy having them visit me."

    a.   manners
    b.   manner
    c.   mannered
    d.   mannerly

16. "I think that the Smiths were embarrassed by Jane's generosity."
"She insisted _____ it as a gift."

    a.   on them to accept
    b.   their accepting
    c.   that they accept
    d.   that they accepted

17. "_____ left your purse in the car?"
"No. I'm sure that I had it with me in the restaurant."

    a.   Might you have
    b.   Might have you
    c.   Have you might
    d.   Had you might

18. "Jim told Alice that he was sorry."
"I was hoping that he _____."

    a.   may
    b.   will
    c.   would
    d.   did

19. "We're late already!"
"You go ahead, and I'll stay here to wait _____."
   a. she
   b. for she
   c. her
   d. for her

20. "Who won the Superbowl football game?"
"Houston. Haven't you been _____ the news?"
   a. listened
   b. listening
   c. listening to
   d. listen

21. "I thought that Larry was a student at State University."
"He is. _____ the day he drives a city bus, and at night he goes to school."
   a. In
   b. During
   c. By
   d. At

22. "Does your family call you very often?"
"Yes, my mother calls about once a week and _____."
   a. so my brother does
   b. so does my brother
   c. my brother does so
   d. my brother so does

23. "How do you know that they were discussing your family?"
"Because they stopped _____ when I entered the room."
   a. to talk
   b. talking
   c. from to talk
   d. from talking

24. "What's bothering you, Kathy?"
"I'm worried _____ taking my oral exams for the Ph.D."
   a. about
   b. of
   c. that
   d. to

25. "Are you busy?"
"We're just _____ ready to go out."
   a. being
   b. doing
   c. having
   d. getting

26. "Joe doesn't seem like the same person."
"_____ so much in the war has made him more thoughtful."
   a. Having seen
   b. Had seen
   c. Have seen
   d. Seen

27. "That's a beautiful necklace!"
"Thank you. It _____ by the Navajo Indians."
   a. made
   b. had made
   c. was made
   d. was making

28. "Someone was waiting for you in your office, but he's gone now."
"Don't you know _____?"
   a. who it was
   b. who was it
   c. who was
   d. who it

29. "Do you believe that James will apologize to Mary?"
"I don't know. He _____."
   a. should
   b. will
   c. ought
   d. owes

30. "Alice has really gained a lot of weight."
"She _____ to go on a diet."
   a. is going
   b. is used
   c. have
   d. must

31. "Did you like my friend?"
"Very much. She's _____ charming as you said she was."

   a. as
   b. very
   c. more
   d. too

32. "Your friend speaks English very well, doesn't she?"
"Yes, she _____ English since she was a little girl."

   a. has been speaking
   b. spoken
   c. used to speak
   d. has to speak

33. "They don't have much in their apartment yet."
"_____ they're plannng to live here only until Bob gets his degree, they don't want to buy much furniture."

   a. Even
   b. Since
   c. Otherwise
   d. However

34. "Did you take enough money with you?"
"No, I needed _____ more than I thought I would."

   a. much
   b. many
   c. any
   d. of

35. "Which woman are you going to vote for?"
"I'm not sure. Everyone says that Joan is _____."

   a. smartest
   b. more smart
   c. the smarter
   d. more smarter

36. "What does the letter say?"
"_____ is the I-20 form that you requested from the University of Tennessee."

   a. Enclosing
   b. Enclose
   c. Enclosed
   d. Enclosure

37. "How did you get along with Miss Evans?"
"_____ us about her dog was a big help."

   a. Your warn
   b. Your warning
   c. You warn
   d. You warning

38. "You've been sick quite a few times since you arrived."
"I just can't _____ to the cold weather."

   a. have used
   b. get used
   c. be used
   d. used

39. "Too bad Mary doesn't like to swim, since she has such a nice pool at her apartment building."
"Her roommate uses it _____ Mary doesn't."

   a. even
   b. even that
   c. even if
   d. even so

40. "Did you say good-bye to Betty?"
"Yes. She gave us her house key just before she _____ so that we could take care of her plants."

   a. has left
   b. left
   c. leaves
   d. leaving

Part II—Vocabulary

Directions

There are forty problems in this part, with four possible answers for each problem. The problems consist of sentences of two types. In Definition Sentences, a word or phrase is underlined. After you read the sentence, read the four possible answers, (a), (b), (c), and (d). Choose the one that is the best definition of the underlined word or phrase. In Completion Sentences, a word or phrase is missing. After you read the sentence, read the four possible answers, (a), (b), (c), and (d). Choose the one that would best complete the sentence.

Don't stop after you finish this part. Continue to Part III.

41. The European Common Market is an association of nations established to encourage trade among members.

    a. allegiance
    b. alliance
    c. allowance
    d. appliance

42. Because the soil is so _____, few plants will grow here.

    a. fancy
    b. rusty
    c. windy
    d. sandy

43. Utilities such as the electric company are usually given monopolies.

    a. special equipment
    b. exclusive rights in an area
    c. a great deal of money
    d. few employees

44. Thank you for your _____ while I was in your city.

    a. nationality
    b. personality
    c. generality
    d. hospitality

45. The fishermen took their boat out an hour before sunrise.

    a. dawn
    b. dusk
    c. twilight
    d. noon

46. The ambassador's staff had the greatest esteem for his intelligence.

    a. suspicion
    b. indignation
    c. submission
    d. admiration

47. This is my mother's _____ for pumpkin pie.

    a. prescription
    b. recipe
    c. formula
    d. syllabus

48. The Parthenon is a traditional example of Doric architecture.

    a. sporadic
    b. prosaic
    c. eccentric
    d. classic

49. An interesting hobby can improve the quality of one's life.

    a. enclose
    b. enforce
    c. enrich
    d. enchant

50. Snow _____ is a big problem in some northern cities.

    a. mobilization
    b. promotion
    c. motive
    d. removal

51. According to an old joke, women always desire pickles and ice cream when they are pregnant.

    a. crave
    b. loathe
    c. shun
    d. chill

52. There was a snap just before my telephone call was disconnected.

    a. click
    b. splash
    c. thump
    d. hum

53. A child under eighteen years old must have a legal _____.

    a. guardian
    b. spouse
    c. bachelor
    d. servant

54. Fir trees and pine trees grow in mild climates.

    a. tropical
    b. frigid
    c. temperate
    d. arid

55. After the revolution, the land that had belonged to the upper classes was divided among the people.

    a. military
    b. clergy

    c. nobility
    d. faculty

56. The speakers at the graduation ceremony are always among the most _____ members of the community.

    a. disappointed
    b. distinguished
    c. discouraged
    d. disgusted

57. The weather has been unusually warm for this time of year.

    a. less warm than usual
    b. not warm at all
    c. as warm as usual
    d. more warm than usual

58. Many people at the rock concert were standing in the _____, because there were no seats left.

    a. aisles
    b. bridges
    c. tributaries
    d. altars

59. A cut of meat from a sheep is referred to as _____.

    a. pork
    b. veal
    c. mutton
    d. poultry

60. The little _____ behind the restaurant is not to be used as a parking lot.

    a. alley
    b. kitty
    c. jacket
    d. cabin

61. Although I was not impressed by him at our first meeting, he has since earned my respect.

    a. usual
    b. ultimate
    c. initial
    d. routine

62. The names of the victims were withheld until their <u>family</u> could be informed.

    a. next of kid

    b. next of keg

    c. next of king

    d. next of kin

63. Why don't you take a few days to <u>consider</u> the alternatives before making a decision?

    a. wander

    b. ponder

    c. flounder

    d. bewilder

64. No _____ woman would go alone to a bar like that one.

    a. respectful

    b. respectable

    c. respecting

    d. respective

65. The witness claims that he has no <u>recollection</u> of what happened next.

    a. ability to tell

    b. ability to forget

    c. ability to change

    d. ability to remember

66. The animal escaped by <u>gnawing</u> a hole in its cage.

    a. finding

    b. digging

    c. biting

    d. hiding

67. His right side was _____ because of an injury to his spine.

    a. blind

    b. deaf

    c. paralyzed

    d. mute

68. The British amateur tennis _____ held annually at Wimbledon attracts some of the best players in the world.

    a. argument

    b. tournament

    c. ailment

    d. punishment

69. The price of _____ has gone up, with a corresponding increase in the cost of bacon, ham, and pork.

    a. hens

    b. hogs

    c. cattle

    d. lambs

70. Please <u>stack</u> those boxes by the door.

    a. open

    b. fold

    c. pile

    d. throw

71. Although we don't have a chair like the one you want here in the store, I am sure that there is one in the _____.

    a. booth

    b. warehouse

    c. barn

    d. elevator

72. In behalf of the families of those who were lost in the accident, we <u>implore</u> you to continue the rescue efforts.

    a. beg

    b. permit

    c. help

    d. force

73. For many years, the New York Yankees <u>ruled</u> the world of professional baseball in the United States.

    a. nominated

    b. dominated

    c. designated

    d. fascinated

74. The correct name for a shooting star is a _____.

    a. satellite

    b. galaxy

    c. planet

    d. meteor

75. It was the custom of many American Indians to wear their hair in _____.

a. brains
b. braids
c. bribes
d. brides

76. The probabilities are 8 to 1 that the horse will win.

a. ratios
b. odds
c. fractions
d. percentages

77. In Atlanta, Georgia, there is a shopping and entertainment area beneath the city streets called _____ Atlanta.

a. Underground
b. Overlook
c. Income
d. Outstanding

78. My dog barks when people come to the door, but he is really quite harmless.

a. dangerous
b. gentle
c. quiet
d. sick

79. After the elections, the losing candidate congratulated his _____.

a. controversy
b. opponent
c. variation
d. grudge

80. The *Christian Science Monitor* is a newspaper that focuses on world news more than other newspapers do.

a. ignores
b. emphasizes
c. explains
d. understands

Part III—Reading Comprehension

Directions

In this part, there are four reading passages, with five problems for each passage. In order to answer the problems, you must be able to read for facts and for inferences; that is, you must be able to understand information that is stated and information that is implied.

The problems are of two types. In the first type, Questions, a question is given. After you read the passage and the question, read the four possible answers, (a), (b), (c), and (d). Choose the one that is the best answer to the question. In the second type, Completions, an incomplete sentence is given. After you read the passage and the incomplete sentence, read the four possible answers, (a), (b), (c), and (d). Choose the one that would best complete the sentence.

Don't spend too much time on one passage, or you may not have time to finish the test.

Sequoyah was born about 1770 in the village of Taskigi. He was a Cherokee Indian, and, along with his entire tribe, he was illiterate. As a result of a hunting accident that left him partially crippled, he enjoyed more leisure time than other tribesmen. And he began to ponder the idea that the Indian people might also come to possess the secret of the "talking leaf." Alone in the woods, he spent hours playing with pieces of wood or making odd little marks on one stone with another. Neither his wife nor his friends offered him any encouragement, and many ridiculed him. But Sequoyah was obsessed with his dream of developing an alphabet for the Cherokee language.

At first, Sequoyah tried to give every word a separate character, but eventually he realized the futility of such an approach and settled on assigning one character to each sound. What he achieved twelve years later was a syllabary of eighty-six characters representing all of the sounds of Cherokee. In combination, they produced a written language of remarkable simplicity and effectiveness. It was so simple, in fact, that it could be learned in a few days. Within a matter of months, a population that had been entirely illiterate became almost entirely literate.

As a tribute to this great Indian educator, the tallest trees in North America, the Sierra Redwoods, were given the name Sequoyahs.

81. From this passage, we know that Sequoyah was

   a. a very tall person
   b. a Taskigi Indian
   c. a married man
   d. easily discouraged

82. Sequoyah had more free time than the other tribesmen because he was

   a. developing an alphabet
   b. a hunter
   c. a very old man
   d. crippled

83. Why did Sequoyah spend so much time in the woods?

   a. because he did not have any friends
   b. because he liked to play
   c. because he was experimenting with a system for an alphabet
   d. because he was hunting for food

84. The Cherokee alphabet

   a. had a separate character for each word
   b. had a separate character for each sound
   c. was very complicated to learn
   d. was not accepted by the tribe

85. How long did it take Sequoyah to develop his alphabet?

   a. a few days
   b. several months
   c. twelve years
   d. all of his life

In this experiment, Robert Rosenthal and Lenore Jacobson investigated the way that innocent subjects might be affected by another person's expectations. First, they gave an intelligence test to the entire student body at an unnamed elementary school in the San Francisco area. Then, they selected students at random and told their teachers that the students' tests had shown that they were about to experience a period of rapid learning. Teachers did not change their methods or materials for teaching the designated students, but, at the end of the year, when the test was administered again, first and second graders who had been selected had, in fact, gained twice as many I.Q. points as the other children. The experimenters concluded that they had performed better because they had been given more attention. Teachers had challenged them and had given them more positive reinforcement because they had expected more from them.

86. What was tested in this experiment?

    a.   the influence of I.Q. tests
    b.   the influence of designated teachers
    c.   the influence of teacher expectations
    d.   the influence of teaching methods and materials

87. How were the subjects chosen to participate in the experiment?

    a.   They were selected by their teachers.
    b.   They were selected by the experimenters.
    c.   They agreed to participate.
    d.   They passed a test.

88. The children who were designated for the experiment gained more I.Q. points than the others because they were

    a.   more intelligent
    b.   taught by different teachers
    c.   taught with new materials and methods
    d.   given more encouragement by their teachers

89. Teachers gave the designated children more attention because

    a.   they were not as intelligent as the other children
    b.   they were told to teach them in a different way
    c.   they expected them to learn faster
    d.   they did not want to challenge them

90. What was the conclusion drawn by the experimenters?

    a.   that an intelligent child scores higher on I.Q. tests
    b.   that teachers should use different teaching methods and materials for intelligent children
    c.   that the expectations of teachers influence children's learning
    d.   that the I.Q. test used in San Francisco schools should be changed

Unfortunately, most of the science fiction films of the 1970s were not much influenced by *2001: A Space Odyssey*. Skillfully directed by Stanley Kubrick, *2001*, which appeared in 1968, set new standards for science fiction films. During the next decade, every one of the dozens of science fiction movies released was compared to *2001*, and all but a few were found sadly lacking.

Admittedly, Kubrick had one of the largest budgets ever for a film of this kind, but, in my opinion, much of the movie's power and appeal was achieved through relatively inexpensive means. For example, the musical score, which was adapted in large part from well-known classical compositions, was reinforced by the use of almost kaleidoscopic visual effects, especially during the space travel sequences. Spectacular camera work was edited to correspond precisely to the ebb and flow of the music.

After *2001*, the dominant theme of science fiction films shifted from the adventures of space travel to the problems created on earth by man's mismanagement of the natural environment and the abuse of technology by a totalitarian state. Overpopulation and the accompanying shortages of food prompt the state to impose extraordinary controls on its citizens. No fewer than twenty-nine films were made around this theme in the years between 1970 and 1977, including *Survivors* and *Chronicles*.

In the opinion of this reviewer, until *Star Wars* was released in 1977, science fiction films were reduced to shallow symbolism disguising to a greater or lesser degree a series of repetitive plots. But *Star Wars* was different. It offered us a return to imaginative voyages in space and confrontation with intelligent life on other planets. Unlike the other science fiction films of the decade, *Star Wars* presented technology as having solved rather than aggravated ecological problems. The special effects created to simulate space vehicles hurtling through the blackness of the universe were reminiscent of the artistic standards set by *2001*.

91. In the author's opinion, most of the science fiction films released in the 1970s were

    a. better than *2001: A Space Odyssey*
    b. not as good as *2001: A Space Odyssey*
    c. almost the same as *Star Wars*
    d. better than *Star Wars*

92. The theme of the majority of science fiction films made between 1970 and 1977 was

    a. space travel
    b. life on other planets
    c. ecological problems on earth
    d. wars between the earth and other planets

93. The author believes that the best science fiction movie made in the 1970s was

    a. *2001: A Space Odyssey*
    b. *Survivors*
    c. *Chronicles*
    d. *Star Wars*

94. In the author's opinion, why was *2001* successful?

    a. because its budget was large
    b. because its camera work and musical score were blended artistically
    c. because its plot was repetitive
    d. because its symbolism was very good

95. What does the author most object to in the science fiction movies of the 1970s?

    a. He objects to their camera work.

    b. He does not like their music.

    c. He believes that their stories are too much alike.

    d. He criticizes their special effects.

Although no one is certain why migration occurs, there are several theories. One theory is based upon the premise that prehistoric birds of the Northern Hemisphere were forced south during the Ice Age, when glaciers covered large parts of Europe, Asia, and North America. As the glaciers melted, the birds came back to their homelands, spent the summer, and then went south again as the ice advanced in winter. In time, the migration became a habit, and now, although the glaciers have disappeared, the habit continues.

Another theory proposes that the ancestral home of all modern birds was the tropics. When the region became overpopulated, many species were crowded north. During the summer, there was plenty of food, but during the winter, scarcity forced them to return to the tropics.

A more recent theory, known as photoperiodism, suggests a relationship between increasing daylight and the stimulation of certain glands in the birds' bodies that may prepare them for migration. One scientist has been able to cause midwinter migrations by exposing birds to artificial periods of daylight. He has concluded that changes occur in the bodies of birds due to seasonal changes in the length of daylight.

96. According to one theory, when the glaciers disappeared, birds

    a. stopped migrating

    b. continued migrating

    c. began migrating again

    d. migrated south and stayed there

97. The author states that birds left the tropics because

    a. there was not enough food there in the winter

    b. there were too many birds

    c. there were too many glaciers

    d. there was too much daylight

98. Why did one scientist expose birds to artificial daylight?

    a. to test the relationship between daylight and a disease of the glands common to birds

    b. to test the relationship between daylight and migration

    c. to test the relationship between migration and temperature

    d. to test the relationship between daylight and changes in the season

99. According to the theory of photoperiodism,

    a. birds should migrate in the middle of the winter

    b. longer days cause changes in the bodies of birds

    c. seasonal changes in the length of days do not affect migration

    d. increasing daylight increases the distance of migration

100. This passage supports the belief that
    a. exact reasons for migration are not known
    b. birds migrate because of changes in temperature
    c. the ancestral home of all birds was the tropics
    d. glaciers caused birds to migrate

Answer Sheet—English Language Proficiency
Model Test Three

Name_____ Date_____

Part I—
Grammar

Part II—
Vocabulary

1. a( ) b( ) c( ) d( )	11. a( ) b( ) c( ) d( )	21. a( ) b( ) c( ) d( )	31. a( ) b( ) c( ) d( )	41. a( ) b( ) c( ) d( )	51. a( ) b( ) c( ) d( )	61. a( ) b( ) c( ) d( )	71. a( ) b( ) c( ) d( )
2. a( ) b( ) c( ) d( )	12. a( ) b( ) c( ) d( )	22. a( ) b( ) c( ) d( )	32. a( ) b( ) c( ) d( )	42. a( ) b( ) c( ) d( )	52. a( ) b( ) c( ) d( )	62. a( ) b( ) c( ) d( )	72. a( ) b( ) c( ) d( )
3. a( ) b( ) c( ) d( )	13. a( ) b( ) c( ) d( )	23. a( ) b( ) c( ) d( )	33. a( ) b( ) c( ) d( )	43. a( ) b( ) c( ) d( )	53. a( ) b( ) c( ) d( )	63. a( ) b( ) c( ) d( )	73. a( ) b( ) c( ) d( )
4. a( ) b( ) c( ) d( )	14. a( ) b( ) c( ) d( )	24. a( ) b( ) c( ) d( )	34. a( ) b( ) c( ) d( )	44. a( ) b( ) c( ) d( )	54. a( ) b( ) c( ) d( )	64. a( ) b( ) c( ) d( )	74. a( ) b( ) c( ) d( )
5. a( ) b( ) c( ) d( )	15. a( ) b( ) c( ) d( )	25. a( ) b( ) c( ) d( )	35. a( ) b( ) c( ) d( )	45. a( ) b( ) c( ) d( )	55. a( ) b( ) c( ) d( )	65. a( ) b( ) c( ) d( )	75. a( ) b( ) c( ) d( )
6. a( ) b( ) c( ) d( )	16. a( ) b( ) c( ) d( )	26. a( ) b( ) c( ) d( )	36. a( ) b( ) c( ) d( )	46. a( ) b( ) c( ) d( )	56. a( ) b( ) c( ) d( )	66. a( ) b( ) c( ) d( )	76. a( ) b( ) c( ) d( )
7. a( ) b( ) c( ) d( )	17. a( ) b( ) c( ) d( )	27. a( ) b( ) c( ) d( )	37. a( ) b( ) c( ) d( )	47. a( ) b( ) c( ) d( )	57. a( ) b( ) c( ) d( )	67. a( ) b( ) c( ) d( )	77. a( ) b( ) c( ) d( )
8. a( ) b( ) c( ) d( )	18. a( ) b( ) c( ) d( )	28. a( ) b( ) c( ) d( )	38. a( ) b( ) c( ) d( )	48. a( ) b( ) c( ) d( )	58. a( ) b( ) c( ) d( )	68. a( ) b( ) c( ) d( )	78. a( ) b( ) c( ) d( )
9. a( ) b( ) c( ) d( )	19. a( ) b( ) c( ) d( )	29. a( ) b( ) c( ) d( )	39. a( ) b( ) c( ) d( )	49. a( ) b( ) c( ) d( )	59. a( ) b( ) c( ) d( )	69. a( ) b( ) c( ) d( )	79. a( ) b( ) c( ) d( )
10. a( ) b( ) c( ) d( )	20. a( ) b( ) c( ) d( )	30. a( ) b( ) c( ) d( )	40. a( ) b( ) c( ) d( )	50. a( ) b( ) c( ) d( )	60. a( ) b( ) c( ) d( )	70. a( ) b( ) c( ) d( )	80. a( ) b( ) c( ) d( )

'Continued on next page)

Part III—
Reading Comprehension

81.		85.		89.		93.		97.	
	a( )		a( )		a( )		a( )		a( )
	b( )		b( )		b( )		b( )		b( )
	c( )		c( )		c( )		c( )		c( )
	d( )		d( )		d( )		d( )		d( )
82.	a( )	86.	a( )	90.	a( )	94.	a( )	98.	a( )
	b( )		b( )		b( )		b( )		b( )
	c( )		c( )		c( )		c( )		c( )
	d( )		d( )		d( )		d( )		d( )
83.	a( )	87.	a( )	91.	a( )	95.	a( )	99.	a( )
	b( )		b( )		b( )		b( )		b( )
	c( )		c( )		c( )		c( )		c( )
	d( )		d( )		d( )		d( )		d( )
84.	a( )	88.	a( )	92.	a( )	96.	a( )	100.	a( )
	b( )		b( )		b( )		b( )		b( )
	c( )		c( )		c( )		c( )		c( )
	d( )		d( )		d( )		d( )		d( )

MODEL TEST THREE
ENGLISH LANGUAGE PROFICENCY

100 Questions

75 Minutes

Part I—Grammar

Directions

There are forty problems in this part, with four possible answers for each problem. Each problem is part of a conversation. In each conversation, a word or a phrase is missing. Following the conversation are four possible answers that might be used to complete the conversation. After you read each conversation, read the four possible answers, (a), (b), (c), and (d). Choose the one that would be best used to complete the conversation.

Don't stop after you finish this part. Continue to Part II.

---

1. "May I take a message?"
   "Yes, please _____ him call me when he gets back to the office."

   a. have
   b. has
   c. to have
   d. having

2. "What did you give Linda for her birthday?"
   "We gave her a _____ machine."

   a. sewer
   b. sewing
   c. sew
   d. sewn

3. "Steve never practices the piano anymore."
   "He plays very well, _____."

   a. however
   b. although
   c. still
   d. but

4. "Donna was really upset!"
   "She's not used to _____ told what to do."

   a. been
   b. being
   c. be
   d. was

5. "Without Bill, I doubt that we'll be able to win."
   "Don't worry. He's going to play _____ his injury."

   a. even though
   b. although
   c. in spite of
   d. even

6. "Mrs. Williams can speak Japanese."
   "Yes. But she would rather _____ English with us last night."

   a. speak
   b. spoke
   c. to speak
   d. have spoken

7. "Does your telephone work now?"
"No. It _____ needs to be fixed."

a. already
b. still
c. yet
d. before

8. "Danny is one of the nicest-looking men I know."
"_____ that, he has a great personality."

a. Beside of
b. Besides of
c. Beside
d. Besides

9. "Did Kathy have any ideas for Jim?"
"She suggested that he _____ a card with all of our names on it."

a. send
b. sends
c. to send
d. sending

10. "Sometimes I forget that Charles isn't an American."
"He will have been _____ in the U.S. for ten years when he graduates."

a. lived
b. live
c. living
d. to live

11. "I don't plan to have a garden this year."
"You should at least plant some tomatoes; _____ you'll have to pay two dollars a basket for them."

a. however
b. otherwise
c. although
d. unless

12. "She won't speak to Bill."
"What could he _____ to make her so angry?"

a. says
b. said
c. to say
d. have said

13. "Do you have any more of these briefcases?"
"I'm sorry. We've sold all _____ this one."

a. but
b. for
c. until
d. that

14. "How are you?"
"Since I left my country, I _____ very homesick."

a. am
b. have
c. have been
d. been

15. "I wish I _____ the orientation program yesterday."
"It's too bad that you didn't. We met a lot of people."

a. had attended
b. have attended
c. would attend
d. could attended

16. "That's a nice bike."
"We bought _____ one we could find because we don't plan to use it very much."

a. cheapest
b. a cheapest
c. the cheapest
d. of cheapest

17. "Does Al like hamburgers?"
"Yes. So much _____ that he eats them almost every day."

a. so
b. as
c. to
d. for

18. "Couldn't we talk about it again?"
"There's nothing left _____."

a. say
b. to say
c. to say it
d. say it

19. "Why was Bob so angry with his wife?"
"Because of _____ late."

    a. her to be
    b. her being
    c. she is
    d. she be

20. "Is this the right place to catch the bus to the shopping center?"
"Yes, just be sure _____ the number fourteen."

    a. to take
    b. taking
    c. take
    d. takes

21. "Do you ever plan to move back to Minnesota?"
"No, but I occasionally think _____ my friends there."

    a. visiting
    b. to visit
    c. of visit
    d. of visiting

22. "You should have known that Anne couldn't keep a secret."
"Never again _____ her anything!"

    a. will I tell
    b. I will tell
    c. will tell
    d. I tell

23. "How do you like your new car?"
"We're very _____ with the gas mileage."

    a. pleasing
    b. pleasure
    c. please
    d. pleased

24. "Your pictures are beautiful!"
"We _____ more if we hadn't run out of film."

    a. would take
    b. had taken
    c. will have taken
    d. would have taken

25. "Who is responsible for this?"
"_____ did it, I hope that the police find him."

    a. Who
    b. Whom
    c. Whoever
    d. Whomever

26. "Steve made a reservation already."
"_____ he change his mind, he can cancel it."

    a. Should
    b. Would
    c. If
    d. So

27. "I don't like to talk to Mr. Davis."
"He speaks _____, doesn't he?"

    a. more fast
    b. too much fast
    c. fastly
    d. fast

28. "This coupon _____ fifty cents toward your next purchase."
"Thank you. I'll use it next week."

    a. worths
    b. is worth
    c. worthy
    d. to worth

29. "Is it true that Ed dropped out of school?"
"Yes. Did he tell you _____?"

    a. what the problem was
    b. what was the problem
    c. the problem was what
    d. was what the problem

30. "It was nice talking with you, but I should let you go now."
"Nice talking with you too, Mary. Thank you _____ calling."

    a. for
    b. to
    c. of
    d. from

31. "Which city did you like most?"
"I enjoyed all of the cities on the tour, but the city _____ I enjoyed most was Miami, Florida."

    a. what
    b. that
    c. where
    d. there

32. "Do you have any pets?"
"Yes, I have _____ kittens."

    a. two small black
    b. small two black
    c. two black small
    d. black small two

33. "Mother will probably be tired after work."
"I know. Let's _____ dinner when she gets home."

    a. be preparing
    b. be prepare
    c. to prepare
    d. preparing

34. "Are you ready to leave?"
"I have a _____ money, but I should probably cash a check first."

    a. few
    b. little
    c. few of
    d. little of

35. "Did you get any mail?"
"No, I haven't gotten a letter _____."

    a. a long time before
    b. since a long time
    c. for a long time
    d. a long time

36. "How about _____ me a hand?"
"Sure. I'd be glad to help."

    a. give
    b. to give
    c. giving
    d. gives

37. "What did you want to talk about, Bill?"
"I'm considering _____ home."

    a. go
    b. going
    c. to go
    d. about going

38. "Which restaurant would you like to go to tonight?"
"_____ the places I've been, I enjoyed the restaurant here in the hotel most."

    a. From all
    b. All of
    c. Of all
    d. All

39. "There are two Olympic medalists entered in the competition."
"How could Mike ever hope _____?"

    a. winning
    b. in winning
    c. to win
    d. that he win

40. "What do you think we should do about this problem?"
"In my opinion, we _____ got to talk with the director."

    a. must
    b. will
    c. have
    d. are

Part II—Vocabulary

Directions

There are forty problems in this part, with four possible answers for each problem. The problems consist of sentences of two types. In Definition Sentences, a word or phrase is underlined. After you read the sentence, read the four possible answers, (a), (b), (c), and (d). Choose the one that is the best definition of the underlined word or phrase. In Completion Sentences, a word or phrase is missing. After you read the sentence, read the four possible answers, (a), (b), (c), and (d). Choose the one that would best complete the sentence.

Don't stop after you finish this part. Continue to Part III.

41. The _____ at the highest point in the United States is 20,000 feet at Mt. McKinley in Alaska.

    a. evolution
    b. elevation
    c. evaluation
    d. elaboration

42. Landlords usually require that their _____ sign one-year leases.

    a. spouses
    b. patients
    c. customers
    d. tenants

43. He received an F in the course because he did not follow the correct procedure for dropping it.

    a. method
    b. official
    c. date
    d. payment

44. The army has been ordered to the southern provinces to subdue an uprising.

    a. defeat
    b. assist
    c. inspect
    d. start

45. The _____ meets once a week to practice the music that they will sing on Sunday morning.

    a. chore
    b. choir
    c. core
    d. cheer

46. Our family has annual reunions when everyone meets for a potluck supper at a local park.

    a. daily
    b. weekly
    c. monthly
    d. yearly

47. An editor is responsible for accepting or rejecting _____ for publication.

    a. manuscripts
    b. inscriptions
    c. scriptures
    d. subscribers

48. In American football, the object is to throw down the man carrying the ball.

    a. tickle
    b. trickle
    c. tackle
    d. twinkle

49. The Amish people have many quaint communities in Pennsylvania where they preserve their old traditions.

    a. peaceful
    b. rural
    c. curious
    d. tiny

50. The suspect gave a signed _____ to the police.

    a. confession
    b. confusion
    c. concession
    d. conversation

51. Many of my friends from abroad tell me that we Americans lead a more hurried life.

    a. easy
    b. rapid
    c. happy
    d. safe

52. We barely had time to buy a ticket before the flight.

    a. always
    b. seldom
    c. never
    d. just

53. Pie is usually cut in _____.

    a. cubes
    b. wedges
    c. spheres
    d. cones

54. The guard must see your identification card before he can authorize you to enter.

    a. assist
    b. permit
    c. force
    d. prevent

55. Although she is very beautiful, her haughty disposition prevents her from having many admirers.

    a. melancholy
    b. proud
    c. jealous
    d. obstinate

56. A _____ is a university administrator above a director and below a vice president.

    a. clerk
    b. professor
    c. dean
    d. instructor

57. We were sorry that our supervisor responded to our suggestions with such indifference.

    a. disorganization
    b. disappointment
    c. disagreement
    d. disinterest

58. Most Americans expect others to wait in lines patiently.

    a. for a long time
    b. in a quiet, calm manner
    c. when necessary
    d. without explanation

59. Some people use herbs to treat illness.

    a. diets
    b. exercise
    c. plants
    d. drugs

60. After holding a _____ for many years, he finally forgave her.

    a. grumble
    b. retort
    c. grudge
    d. mistake

61. This apartment is much more <u>spacious</u> than the one where you lived before.

    a. large
    b. beautiful
    c. expensive
    d. comfortable

62. Because of spring rains, the rivers and streams usually <u>flood</u> their banks at this time of year.

    a. overcome
    b. overtake
    c. overflow
    d. oversee

63. Young women from every state _____ for the title of Miss America.

    a. complain
    b. compel
    c. compete
    d. compose

64. The earth is <u>turning</u> on its axis at the rate of once every twenty-three hours, fifty-six minutes.

    a. swelling
    b. shrinking
    c. spinning
    d. speeding

65. Don't be afraid to <u>confide</u> in your lawyer, because he is pledged to keep all information secret.

    a. trust
    b. distrust
    c. agree with
    d. disagree with

66. Pizza places often have _____ service for people who want to eat at home.

    a. delay
    b. display
    c. dreary
    d. delivery

67. To most people, frogs and _____ look very much alike.

    a. mice
    b. lions
    c. toads
    d. apes

68. The President has appointed a commission in order to <u>stimulate</u> interest in learning foreign languages.

    a. study
    b. find
    c. cause
    d. change

69. Near the scene of the crime, the police arrested two men whose behavior appeared _____.

    a. ambitious
    b. gregarious
    c. suspicious
    d. notorious

70. Providing <u>adequate</u> housing for an increasing population is one of the pressing concerns of this decade.

    a. satisfactory
    b. attractive
    c. additional
    d. inexpensive

71. The United Nations must serve as a <u>neutral</u> body in order to help in resolving disputes among member nations.

    a. unique
    b. biased
    c. temporary
    d. impartial

72. Large corporations often have a wide _____ of activities, including business, education, research, and social programs.

    a. tray
    b. frame
    c. scope
    d. lawn

73. Dr. Michael DeBakey is one of the most skillful heart surgeons in the world.

    a. famous
    b. able
    c. busy
    d. unique

74. The rules of grammar may be _____, but often the exceptions do not seem to fit any system.

    a. magical
    b. comical
    c. logical
    d. political

75. We could not sleep because of the vibration of the train.

    a. noise
    b. movement
    c. speed
    d. temperature

76. There was a(n) _____ in the fighting while both sides made plans for the next offensive.

    a. lull
    b. intermission
    c. recess
    d. strike

77. Multiple vitamins usually supply the minimum daily requirements of vitamins A, B, C, E, and iron.

    a. best
    b. least
    c. most
    d. first

78. Nothing ruffles him.

    a. makes him tired
    b. makes him upset
    c. makes him happy
    d. makes him afraid

79. We received a very friendly welcome when we arrived.

    a. cordial
    b. aloof
    c. modest
    d. affected

80. Eclipses of the moon and sun have been predicted with great accuracy since ancient times.

    a. interest
    b. exactness
    c. regularity
    d. agreement

Part III—Reading Comprehension

Directions

In this part, there are four reading passages, with five problems for each passage. In order to answer the problems, you must be able to read for facts and for inferences; that is, you must be able to understand information that is stated and information that is implied.

The problems are of two types. In the first type, Questions, a question is given. After you read the passage and the question, read the four possible answers, (a), (b), (c), and (d). Choose the one that is the best answer to the question. In the second type, Completions, an incomplete sentence is given. After you read the passage and the incomplete sentence, read the four possible answers, (a), (b), (c), and (d). Choose the one that would best complete the sentence.

Don't spend too much time on one passage, or you may not have time to finish the test.

In order to produce commercial records, an original record must first be made. It is a flat disc, usually made of aluminum coated with a soft layer of lacquer. As the disc is rotated, a sapphire or ruby stylus cuts a continuous groove in the lacquer coating. The stylus travels around the disc, making an impression that corresponds to the amplitude and frequency of the sound being recorded. When completed, the original may be played back to re-create the original recorded sound.

If the sound produced by the original record is satisfactory, the original is coated with silver to conduct electricity, and then electroplated with nickel. When the original is stripped away, a negative of the original remains, with a raised spiral pattern corresponding to the grooves in the original. The negative is called a master matrix.

Next, the master matrix is electroplated with nickel to produce a positive of the original. The positive is called a mother matrix. By electroplating the mother matrix with nickel and stripping it away, stampers are produced. Stampers are negatives of the original record from which the final records may be pressed.

One stamper for each side of the record is placed on either side of a hydraulic press. A preform of shellac compound or plastic is placed between the stampers. The press is heated and closed. When an impression of the stampers has been made in the material, the press is quickly cooled and opened. The grooves in the finished record correspond to those in the original lacquer disc.

81. What is the purpose of silver in making commercial records?

    a. It strips away the original record.

    b. It cuts a groove in the original record.

    c. It aids in electroplating the original record.

    d. It makes an impression on the stamper.

82. The mother matrix is a(n)

    a. negative of the original record

    b. stamper

    c. original record

    d. record made from a master matrix

83. Why is lacquer used to coat the aluminum disc?

    a. because it conducts electricity

    b. because it can be cut by a stylus

    c. because it cools quickly

    d. because it protects the impression in the aluminum

84. Preforms are made of

    a. nickel or silver
    b. sapphire or ruby
    c. shellac or plastic
    d. aluminum or lacquer

85. Commercial records are made directly from a(n)

    a. original record
    b. master matrix
    c. mother matrix
    d. stamper

In August, 1869, Wild Bill Hickok was elected sheriff of Ellis County, Kansas, where he soon developed a reputation as one of the best gunmen and most colorful characters in all of the territory.

A rowdy, boastful man, Wild Bill had a unique physical appearance that contributed significantly to his fame. While most of his fellow lawmen favored informal clothes, Bill was a notorious dandy. He was fond of elegantly tailored European-style suits with fancy satin lapels, ruffled shirts, and colorful silk ties. Along with the two guns that he carried in holsters on either side of his belt, he sported a knife that he tied around his waist in a bright red sash. But his most striking feature was his yellow hair. He wore it shoulder-length and carefully formed into curls that were kept in place by fragrant hair oil. His long, drooping moustache was waxed, and it twirled up at the ends.

Once, as sheriff of Ellis County, Bill was pursuing two outlaws. As they fled in opposite directions, he fired at the two simultaneously and killed them both. On another occasion, after bragging that he could shoot more than one hole in a hat that had been thrown in the air, he shot a row of evenly-spaced holes along the edge of the brim before the hat hit the ground.

86. The person described was

    a. European
    b. a tailor
    c. a lawman
    d. an outlaw

87. The feature that most distinguished Wild Bill Hickok was his

    a. knife
    b. hat
    c. moustache
    d. hair

88. From this passage, we know that Wild Bill Hickok was not

    a. famous
    b. elegant
    c. boastful
    d. informal

89. Where did Wild Bill Hickok carry his knife?

    a. in his belt
    b. in his shirt
    c. in a sash
    d. in a set of holsters

90. Why did Wild Bill Hickok shoot holes in a hat?

    a. because he was pursuing two outlaws
    b. because he wanted to prove that he could do it
    c. because he was trying to kill the man wearing the hat
    d. because he did not like the hat

The cost of health care in the United States has increased tenfold during the last twenty-five years, tripled during the last ten years, and doubled during the last five years. In 1970, one night in an average American hospital cost $75. By 1980, the same hospital was charging $200. Intensive care cost more than $300. Today hospital charges for surgery and post-operative care can easily reach $10,000, including $3,000 for the surgeon and $700 for the anesthesiologist.

One reason that the cost is so high can be traced to advances in medical technology that include expensive equipment and highly-trained, highly-paid personnel to run it. As an example, the CAT, a computerized scanner used for diagnostic purposes, now costs $600,000.

The problem is all the more serious because, unlike many other countries, the U.S. does not have a national health insurance plan.

91. According to the passage, new medical technology

    a. has no effect on the high cost of health care
    b. contributes to the high cost of health care
    c. may solve some of the problems related to the high cost of health care
    d. requires less highly-trained, less highly-paid personnel

92. In 1980, one night in a regular hospital room cost

    a. $75
    b. $200
    c. $300
    d. $700

93. Over the last ten years, the cost of health care in the U.S. has increased

    a. twenty-five times
    b. ten times
    c. three times
    d. two times

94. The CAT is used as an example of

    a. intensive care
    b. health insurance
    c. medical equipment
    d. hospital personnel

95. According to the author of this passage, how is the United States different from other countries?

   a. The United States has more hospitals.
   b. The United States has better doctors.
   c. The United States does not have a national insurance plan for health care.
   d. The United States does not have a computerized scanner for diagnostic purposes.

From the top of the famous Hyatt Regency Hotel in Atlanta, you will see a dramatic view of this beautiful city—toward the south, the South Expressway leading to Hartsfield-Atlanta International Airport, the second busiest airport in the country; in the foreground, Peachtree Street, a canyon of modern skyscrapers in glass and steel. The tallest building in the skyline, the First National Bank Building, is surrounded by other giants—the New Trust Company Building, the Equitable Life Building, and the Peachtree Center, a complex that contains the largest merchandise mart in the South.

Just beyond the business district, you will see the shining dome of the State Capitol Building, made of twenty-four-karat gold. To the right of the capitol are rows of white marble office buildings; farther south is the Atlanta Stadium; and not quite out of sight is the Farmer's Market, the largest wholesale fresh fruit and vegetable center in the South.

96. The dome of the State Capitol is made of

   a. glass
   b. steel
   c. gold
   d. marble

97. Which building is the tallest?

   a. the Hyatt Regency Hotel
   b. the First National Bank Building
   c. the Peachtree Center
   d. the State Capitol

98. Where is the largest merchandise mart in the South?

   a. at the International Airport
   b. at the Farmer's Market
   c. at the Peachtree Center
   d. at the Hyatt Regency Hotel

99. The South Expressway leads to

   a. Atlanta Stadium
   b. the Farmer's Market
   c. Atlanta International Airport
   d. Peachtree Street

100. How does the author feel about the city?

   a. He criticizes the architecture of the buildings.
   b. He praises the view of the city.
   c. He compares it with Hartsfield.
   d. He compares it with cities in the North.

expletives call attention to the subject. The verb *be* is usually used after an expletive; it agrees in number (singular or plural) with the subject.

34. **c** *Children* is the plural form of the noun *child*.

35. **b** *So* must be used with *that* to express cause and effect. "She was *very* upset" would also be correct.

36. **a** *Had*, a subject, and a participle, in that order, must be used to express a condition. "*If John had been there*" would also be correct.

37. **c** The relative pronoun *what* must be used in a clause in which something is left unidentified. Remember, *what* means *that which*.

38. **a** An adjective must be used after the verb *to taste*. Choice (b) is an adverb. Choice (c) is a noun. Choice (d) is ungrammatical; there is no such word as *freshing*.

39. **b** *Can* must be used to express ability. Remember, *can* means *to be able*.

40. **b** The possessive pronoun *his* must be used to refer to the possessive question word *whose*.

41. **a** A *precaution* is an action taken to avoid a future accident or problem. All of the other choices have some sounds like those in the word *precaution*, but they have different meanings. Choice (b) means a conference. Choice (c) means ruin. Choice (d) means disappointment or discouragement.

42. **d** A *refusal* is a negative reply. All of the other choices have some sounds like those in the word *refusal*, but they have different meanings. Choice (a) means a release, especially from employment. Choice (b) means a separation or elimination. Choice (c) means acceptance or admiration.

43. **a** A *variation* is a difference. Choice (b) means a likeness. Choice (c) means a difference in opinion. Choice (d) means a likeness in opinion. Choice (b) is the opposite of choice (a). Choice (d) is the opposite of choice (c).

44. **c** *Virtuous* means honorable. All of the other choices have some sounds like those in the word *virtuous*, but they have different meanings. Choice (a) means dull or boring. Choice (b) means noticeable or easy to see. Choice (d) means famous.

45. **a** *Obedient* means willing to follow orders or commands. All of the other choices have some sounds like those in the word *obedient*, but they have different meanings. Choice (b) means indebted. Choice (c) means stubborn. Choice (d) means old or no longer used.

46. **c** A *successor* is one who comes after. All of the other choices have some sounds like those in the word *successor*, but they have different meanings. Choice (a) is an affix added to the end of a word to form a new word; for example, *ness* is a *suffix* added to the word *sad* to form *sadness*. Choice (b) means something added to a complete written work. Choice (d) means a continuation of an earlier work.

47. **a** *Mutual* means similar or shared. All of the other choices have some sounds like those in the word *mutual*, but they have different meanings. Choice (b) means not usual or not common. Choice (c) means made of two parts. Choice (d) means friendly.

48. **d** *Sane* means rational. All of the other choices have some sounds like those in the word *sane*, but they have different meanings. Choice (a) means useless or proud and haughty. Choice (b) means gentle or domesticated. Choice (c) means crippled.

49. **b** To *quicken* means to increase. Choice (a) means to begin. Choice (c) means to slow. Choice (d) means to end. Choice (c) is the opposite of choice (b). Choice (d) is the opposite of choice (a).

50. c *Shelves* are storage spaces for books and other small objects. All of the other choices also refer to storage, but they are containers which things are stored *in*, not spaces which things are stored *on*. Choice (a) means a large wooden box. Choice (b) means a large hard-sided suitcase. Choice (d) means a woven container, often made of straw or wood.

51. c *Forbidden* means prohibited. Choice (b) means permitted or supported. Choice (b) is the opposite of choice (c). The other two choices are not definitions of the word *forbidden*. Choice (a) means praised. Choice (d) means accompanied.

52. a A *trumpet* is a musical instrument. All of the other choices have some sounds like those in the word *trumpet*, but they have different meanings. Choice (b) means a group of four, especially four musicians. Choice (c) means a frying pan. Choice (d) means a cupboard with shelves and drawers.

53. d *Specimens* are examples. All of the other choices have some sounds like those in the word *specimens*, but they have different meanings. Choice (a) means an observer, especially of a sporting event. Choice (b) means a distinct category of plant or animal. Choice (c) means a range of related qualities, ideas, or events.

54. d To *overthrow* means to defeat, especially a government. All of the other choices have some sounds like those in the word *overthrow*, but they have different meanings. Choice (a) means to charge too much. Choice (b) means to do too much. Choice (c) means to ignore or to not notice.

55. a To *sneak* means to move quietly and secretly. None of the other choices is a definition of the word *sneak*. Choice (b) means pure. Choice (c) means hasty or reckless. Choice (d) means to tell funny stories or to jest.

56. b *Nominated* means named. None of the other choices is a definition of the word *nominated*. Choice (a) means studied or taken into account. Choice (c) means denied or rejected. Choice (d) means debated or talked about.

57. a To *suppress* means to hide. Choice (b) means to demonstrate. Choice (b) is the opposite of choice (a). The other two choices are not definitions of the word *suppress*. Choice (c) means to bring about or to effect. Choice (d) means to accept as true.

58. d A *pint* is a liquid unit of measurement equal to sixteen ounces. All of the other choices also refer to measurements, but they are not equal to sixteen ounces. Choice (a) is equal to one unit on a scale of temperature. Choice (b) is equal to 4840 square yards of land. Choice (c) is equal to 2000 pounds of weight.

59. b *Pensions* are regular payments, especially to retired or disabled persons. All of the other choices refer to payments also, but not payments given to retired persons. Choice (a) means payment for work. Choice (c) means payment in return for investment in a business. Choice (d) means payment for a special service or deed.

60. b To *jam* means to crowd. None of the other choices is a definition of the word *jam*. Choice (a) means to travel without destination. Choice (c) means to scatter or to spread out. Choice (d) means to run with short, bouncing steps.

61. a To *ripen* means to mature, especially in reference to fruit. All of the other choices describe stages of maturity, but they do not define the word *mature*. Choice (b) means to blossom. Choice (c) means to die. Choice (d) means to gather a crop.

62. b An *isthmus* is a narrow strip of land connecting two larger bodies of land. All of the other choices also refer to bodies of land, but not to narrow connecting strips. Choice (a) means a body of land with water on three sides. (The state of Florida is a

peninsula.) Choice (c) means a body of land with water on all sides. (The state of Hawaii is made up of several *islands*.) Choice (d) means one of the seven major bodies of land in the world. (North America is a *continent*.)

63. **b** To *rap* means to strike or to knock. All of the other choices also refer to striking, but not to knocking on a door. Choice (a) means to strike with an open hand, especially as a punishment. Choice (c) means to strike both hands together, especially as applause after a performance. Choice (d) means to strike very gently with an open hand, especially as an expression of affection.

64. **b** *Tragic* means unfortunate. None of the other choices is a definition of the word *tragic*. Choice (a) means rapid or abrupt. Choice (c) means well-known or celebrated. Choice (d) means odd or eccentric.

65. **c** *Shrubs* are bushes. All of the other choices have some sounds like those in the word *shrubs*, but they have different meanings. Choice (a) means a gesture of doubt or indifference made by raising the shoulders. Choice (b) means an area shielded from light, such as the ground under a leafy tree. Choice (d) means a sacred or holy place, especially the tomb of a saint.

66. **d** A *plea* is a statement of defense. All of the other choices also refer to statements, but not to statements of defense. Choice (a) means a statement that resolves a problem. Choice (b) means a statement that proves ownership of purchase. Choice (c) means a statement that repeats an original statement.

67. **c** *Crumbs* are small pieces of pastry, especially cake or bread. All of the other choices also refer to small pieces, but not to pieces of bread. Choice (a) means a small piece of fruit or vegetable skin. Choice (b) means a small piece of cloth or of anything left over. Choice (d) means a small amount of solid sediment at the bottom of a container of coffee.

68. **b** A *dependent* is a person for whom another is responsible. None of the other choices is a definition of the word *dependent*. Choice (a) means a citizen who owes allegiance to a monarch or ruler. Choice (c) means a prisoner. Choice (d) means an administrator or a manager.

69. **b** A *serpent* is a snake or a viper. Choice (a) has some sounds like those in the word *serpent*, but it means an employee hired to perform domestic service, like a maid or a cook. Choices (c) and (d) have some sounds like those in the word *viper*, but they have different meanings. Choice (c) means energy or strength. Choice (d) means mist or fog.

70. **c** *Serene* means calm. All of the other choices also refer to expressions of emotion, but not to calm. Choice (a) means irritated or displeased. Choice (b) means afraid. Choice (d) means content or glad.

71. **b** To *converse* means to talk. All of the other choices describe situations in which it would be appropriate to converse, but they do not define the word *converse*. Choice (a) means to encounter. Choice (c) means to negotiate or to bargain. Choice (d) means to journey.

72. **a** *Interference* is interruption, especially in an uninvited or unwelcome way. None of the other choices is a definition of the word *interference*. Choice (b) means a donation. Choice (c) means an official paper. Choice (d) means a purpose or a goal.

73. **c** *Lasting* means permanent. None of the other choices is a definition of the word *lasting*. Choice (a) means distressful. Choice (b) means surprising. Choice (d) means offensive.

74. a   *Dungeons* are prisons, especially the underground prisons found in medieval castles. All of the other choices also refer to medieval times, but not to prisons. Choice (b) means a fortified residence. Choice (c) means a small town or a village. Choice (d) means a king or a ruler.

75. b   *Fragrances* are pleasant smells, especially perfumes. All of the other choices also refer to the senses, but not to the sense of smell. Choice (a) refers to taste. Choice (c) refers to sound. Choice (d) refers to sight.

76. d   *Expansion* is an extension of territory or authority. All of the other choices have some sounds like those in the word *expansion*, but they have different meanings. Choice (a) means a trip. Choice (b) means a violent release of energy as when a bomb goes off. Choice (c) means the condition of dying out, especially in reference to a group of animals.

77. a   To *revive* means to return to life or consciousness. All of the other choices have some sounds like those in the word *revive*, but they have different meanings. Choice (b) means to improve. Choice (c) means to change, especially a written work. Choice (d) means to change, especially a direction or a decision.

78. b   To *install* means to put in, especially an appliance. All of the other choices have some sounds like those in the word *install*, but they have different meanings. Choice (a) means to protect. Choice (c) means to teach, especially moral or ethical values. Choice (d) means to examine.

79. b   *Stricken* means affected by a strong emotion, trouble, or illness. All of the other choices have some sounds like those in the word *stricken*, but they have different meanings. Choice (a) means difficult to change. Choice (c) means absolute, severe, or rigid. Choice (d) means strong.

80. a   *Gigantic* means large. All of the other choices may describe the park, but they do not define the word *gigantic*. Choice (b) means costly. Choice (c) means pretty or attractive. Choice (d) means recent.

81. d   "Unlike antibiotics, interferon does not attack germs directly" (paragraph 3). Choice (a) contradicts the fact that interferon has provoked no negative reaction of sufficient significance to discourage its use. Choice (b) contradicts the fact that last year only one gram of interferon was produced in the entire world. Choice (c) contradicts the fact that interferon is so potent that the amount given to each patient is very small.

82. b   ". . . it [interferon] makes unaffected cells resistant to infection . . ." (paragraph 3). Choices (a) and (c) are not mentioned, and may not be concluded from information in the passage. Choice (d) contradicts the fact that interferon does not attack germs directly.

83. c   "The drug [interferon] is produced by infecting white blood cells with a virus" (paragraph 2). Although interferon is a protein used in the treatment of viruses, bacteria, and tumors, choices (a), (b), and (d) are not mentioned as ways of producing interferon.

84. c   ". . . last year only one gram [of interferon] was produced in the entire world" (paragraph 1). Choice (a) contradicts the fact that interferon has not provoked any negative reaction. Choice (b) contradicts the fact that a large-scale project is now underway in the United States. Choice (d) contradicts the fact that, to treat human beings, interferon produced by human beings must be used.

85. d   "The survival rate over a three-year period was 70 percent among those who were treated with interferon" (paragraph 4). Choice (a) contradicts the fact that 70 percent, not 50 percent, of the patients reacted favorably. Half of the patients in the

study were given interferon and half were given conventional treatments. Choice (b) contradicts the fact that 10 to 30 percent of those patients who had received conventional treatments were still alive after three years. Choice (c) is improbable, since the purpose of the study was to compare the effects of conventional treatments and interferon on different groups of patients.

86. **d** "In fact, it was Dawes who rode first, rode longer, and performed the task better" (paragraph 2). Choice (a) refers to the poet who wrote "Paul Revere's Ride," not to the man who alerted the colonists. Choice (b) refers to the man who has received the most credit, not to the man who should receive it. Choice (c) refers to the commander who sent the riders to alert the colonists.

87. **b** ". . . in April of 1775, Commander Joseph Warren sent two young men out on horseback to alert the American rebels between Boston and Lexington that the British were coming . . ." (paragraph 2); ". . . thereby . . . sparking the Revolutionary War at Lexington" (paragraph 1). The dates for choices (a), (c), and (d) are not mentioned and may not be concluded from information in the passage.

88. **c** "In Henry Wadsworth Longfellow's fanciful poem . . . complete credit was given to Paul Revere . . . Although an utter corruption of truth, the myth has persisted . . ." (paragraph 1). Choices (a) and (b) are correct, but neither is the reason that Revere was remembered. Choice (d) is not mentioned, and may not be concluded from information in the passage.

89. **b** ". . . the Revolutionary War at Lexington" (paragraph 1). Choice (a) refers to the country engaged in the war with America, not to the country in which the war began. Choice (c) refers to the nickname of the American soldiers. Choice (d) refers to the city where Revere and Dawes began their ride.

90. **d** "In fact, it was Dawes who rode first, rode longer, and performed the task better" (paragraph 2). Choice (a) contradicts the fact that Revere was captured near the end of his ride. Choice (b) contradicts the fact that Dawes performed the task better. Choice (c) contradicts the fact that Revere, not Dawes, got lost.

91. **c** ". . . there are exceptions to spelling patterns, which must be learned one word at a time" (paragraph 2). Choice (a) refers to the opinion of other educators, not to that of the author. Choice (b) contradicts the fact that the author suggests learning the exceptions one word at a time. Choice (d) is not mentioned, and may not be concluded from information in the passage. The book does not teach you how to use a dictionary.

92. **b** 'I [the author] believe that . . . patterns will help you" (paragraph 2). Choice (a) refers to the best way to learn exceptions, not all words. Choices (c) and (d) are improbable, because the author states that they are not the purpose of the book.

93. **d** "Its [the book's] main objective is to introduce regular spelling patterns; that is, to present a regular system for spelling a large group of words" (paragraph 1). Choices (a) and (c) contradict the fact that the book does not treat either the complex rules of English orthography or the way to use a dictionary. Choice (b) is not mentioned, and may not be concluded from information in the passage.

94. **b** "By learning these patterns, and by practicing them, students will master thousands of words" (paragraph 1). Choices (a) and (d) are improbable, because the objective of the book is to present a system for spelling a large group of words, not all English words or all English words in the dictionary. Choice (c) contradicts the fact that the exceptions must be learned one word at a time.

95. **c** ". . . unlike some educators, I do not believe that learning to spell English is an

impossible task" (paragraph 2). Since the phrase "unlike some educators" is used, it must be concluded that other educators disagree with the author. Choices (a) and (b) contradict the fact that other educators disagree with the author. Choice (d) contradicts the fact that the author does not believe that spelling is impossible.

96. b ". . . Edwin Link had found an anchor that he believed might belong to the flagship *[Santa Maria]*" (paragraph 2). Choice (a) refers to Fred Dickson, not to Edwin Link. Choices (c) and (d) refer to people who were not mentioned by name in the passage.

97. d "Probably the most significant find was some pottery . . ." (paragraph 2). Choice (a) refers to a significant find from a later expedition, not from the first expedition. Choice (b) refers to a find from the first expedition, but not to the most significant find. Choice (c) refers to a find from Link's expedition, not Dickson's expedition.

98. b ". . . and a few silver nails, presumably from a piece of armor" (paragraph 2). Choices (a), (c), and (d) are not mentioned, and may not be concluded from information in the passage.

99. c "Dickson discovered an object about seventy-five feet southeast of the coral reef. . . That it was a ship was certain" (paragraph 4). Choices (a) and (d) refer to the place where Dickson's crew had been working before they discovered the ship. Choice (b) is not mentioned as the site of a find. The ship found was one hundred feet long.

100. c "That it was a ship was certain. Whether it was the *Santa Maria* is still an open question" (paragraph 4). Since it is still an open question, the ship may or may not be the *Santa Maria*. Choice (a) contradicts the fact that it may not be the *Santa Maria*. Choice (b) contradicts the fact that it may be the *Santa Maria*. Choice (d) contradicts the fact that it was a ship.

Model Test Two

Answer Key

1.	b	21.	b	41.	b	61.	c	81.	c
2.	a	22.	b	42.	d	62.	d	82.	d
3.	a	23.	b	43.	b	63.	b	83.	c
4.	c	24.	a	44.	d	64.	b	84.	b
5.	b	25.	d	45.	a	65.	d	85.	c
6.	c	26.	a	46.	d	66.	c	86.	c
7.	a	27.	c	47.	b	67.	c	87.	b
8.	b	28.	a	48.	d	68.	b	88.	d
9.	d	29.	a	49.	c	69.	b	89.	c
10.	c	30.	a	50.	d	70.	c	90.	c
11.	b	31.	a	51.	a	71.	b	91.	b
12.	a	32.	a	52.	a	72.	a	92.	c
13.	a	33.	b	53.	a	73.	b	93.	d
14.	c	34.	a	54.	c	74.	d	94.	b
15.	c	35.	c	55.	c	75.	b	95.	c
16.	c	36.	c	56.	b	76.	b	96.	b
17.	a	37.	b	57.	d	77.	a	97.	b
18.	c	38.	b	58.	a	78.	b	98.	b
19.	d	39.	c	59.	c	79.	b	99.	b
20.	c	40.	b	60.	a	80.	b	100.	a

Explanatory Answers

1. b *The one* must be used to refer to the singular noun *house*. "That's *it*" would also be correct.

2. a An object pronoun must be used in the complement after the verb *to give*.

3. a *Have been* and an *-ing* verb form must be used to express a continuous activity. The verb *has* must be used for agreement with the pronoun *she*. *For* or *since* is usually used with continuous activity.

4. c *Could*, a subject, and *have*, in that order, must be used in a question. "*Could* they *have worried* about their son?" would also be correct.

5. b *Be* and an *-ing* verb form must be used with the adverb *now* to express an activity in progress. "I *check* it *every day*" would also be correct.

6. c *As* must be used with *so*. Remember, *so long as* means *if*.

7. a *It* must be used between the first and second words in the separable two-word verb *to look up*. Remember, *to look up* means *to refer to [something] in a source*, especially in a book.

8. b An object pronoun must be used in the complement.

9. **d** The adjective phrase *all kinds of* must be used with the plural noun *sports*.

10. **c** *Were* and a participle must be used to express a passive. Remember, passive verbs are used to emphasize the object of the active sentence. The active sentence "The news surprised *us*" would also be correct.

11. **b** An auxiliary, subject, and main verb, in that order, must be used after an initial negative like *never*.

12. **a** An imperative form must be used with the conjunction *and*. "*If* you pay my way, I'll be glad to go" would also be correct.

13. **a** *Of all* must be used to express selection. Remember, *of all* means *from among all*.

14. **c** *Since* must be used to express cause. Remember, one of the meanings of *since* is *because*.

15. **c** An adjective must be used to modify the noun *children*. Choices (a) and (b) are nouns. Choice (d) is an adjective, but it cannot be used with the adverb *well*.

16. **c** A verb word (simple verb) must be used in the clause after the verb *to insist*.

17. **a** *Might*, a subject, and *have*, in that order, must be used in a question.

18. **c** *Would* must be used in the clause after a past form of the verb *to hope*.

19. **d** The preposition *for* must be used after the verb *to wait*. An object pronoun must be used after the preposition.

20. **c** An *-ing* verb form must be used after the participle *been*. The preposition *to* must be used with the verb *to listen* before a noun phrase.

21. **b** *During* must be used with *the day*. "*In the daytime*" and "*by day*" would also be correct.

22. **b** *So* must be used with an auxiliary and a subject, in that order, to express agreement. "My brother does, *too*" would also be correct.

23. **b** An *-ing* verb form must be used after the verb *to stop*.

24. **a** The preposition *about* must be used after the verb *to worry*.

25. **d** *Get ready* must be used to express preparation. Remember, *to get ready* means *to prepare; to be ready* means *to be prepared*.

26. **a** An *-ing* verb form must be used as a noun phrase subject. A participle must be used after *having*. "Because he has *seen* so much in the war, he is more thoughtful" would also be correct.

27. **c** *Was* and a participle must be used to express a passive. Remember, passive verbs are used to emphasize the object of the active sentence. The active sentence "The Navajo Indians made *it*" would also be correct.

28. **a** A subject and a verb, in that order, must be used in the clause after a question word.

29. **a** *Should* must be used to express obligation or responsibility. "*He ought to*" would also be correct.

30. **a** Be *going to* must be used to express future action. Remember, *going to* means *will*. "She is *used to going* on a diet" and "she *must go* on a diet" would also be correct.

31. **a** The adverb *as* must be used with *as* to compare equals. "She's *more* charming *than* you said" and "She's *very* charming" would also be correct.

32. **a** *Have been* and an *-ing* verb form must be used to express a continuous activity. The

verb *has* must be used for agreement with the pronoun *she*. *For* and *since* are usually used with continuous activity.

33. **b** *Since* must be used to express cause. Remember, one of the meanings of *since* is *because*.

34. **a** The adverb *much* must be used with the adjective *more* to refer to the non-count noun *money*.

35. **a** An *-er* form with a one-syllable adjective must be used to compare two people. "Joan is *the* smart*est*" would also be correct, if three or more people were being compared.

36. **c** An adjective must be used to modify the subject *the I-20 form*. Choice (b) is a verb. Choice (d) is a noun. Choice (a) is an adjective, but it would refer to the person who enclosed the form, not to the I-20 form. Remember, an *-ed* adjective is used to express an effect; an *-ing* adjective is used to express a cause.

37. **b** An *-ing* form must be used as a noun phrase subject. A possessive pronoun such as *your* must be used with an *-ing* form.

38. **b** *Get used to* must be used to express custom. Remember, *to get used to* means *to become accustomed to*.

39. **c** *Even if* must be used to express concession. Remember, *even if* means *even though*, *although*.

40. **b** A simple past form must be used to refer to one specific time in the past.

41. **b** An *alliance* is an association, especially an association among nations. All of the other choices have some sounds like those in the word *alliance*, but they have different meanings. Choice (a) means loyalty. Choice (c) means a regular payment of money or food, usually to a dependent. Choice (d) means a small machine, especially for household use.

42. **d** *Sandy* means made of sand or similar to sand. Sand is very fine particles of rock, a little coarser than dirt. All of the other choices have some sounds like those in the word *sandy*, but they have different meanings. Choice (a) means elegant. Choice (b) means oxidized. Choice (c) means breezy or gusting.

43. **b** *Monopolies* are organizations that have exlusive rights. The phrases in choices (a), (c), and (d) may describe monopolies, but they do not define them. The most important characteristic of a monopoly is that of exclusive rights or control over competition.

44. **d** *Hospitality* is the act of making guests welcome, especially in one's home. All of the other choices have some sounds like those in the word *hospitality*, but they have different meanings. Choice (a) means citizenship. Choice (b) means character. Choice (c) means an observation with general application.

45. **a** *Dawn* is sunrise. All of the other choices also refer to times of day, but not to dawn. Choices (b) and (c) refer to evening, just before sunset. Choice (d) refers to midday.

46. **d** *Esteem* is admiration. None of the other choices is a definition of the word *esteem*. Choice (a) means doubt. Choice (b) means anger. Choice (c) means obedience.

47. **b** A *recipe* is a set of directions for preparing food. All of the other choices refer to directions, but not to directions for the preparation of pie. Choice (a) means a set of directions for preparing medicine or drugs. Chcice (c) means a set of directions for preparing mathematical statements, or for preparing food for infants. Choice (d) means a set of directions for teaching a course of studies.

48. **d** *Classic* means traditional. All of the other choices have some sounds like those in the

word *classic*, but they have different meanings. Choice (a) means irregular. Choice (b) means ordinary or direct. Choice (c) means strange.

49.   c   To *enrich* means to improve the quality of something. All of the other choices have some sounds like those in the word *enrich*, but they have different meanings. Choice (a) means to contain or to confine. Choice (b) means to compel obedience. Choice (d) means to charm or to delight.

50.   d   *Removal* is disposal. None of the other choices is a definition of the word *removal*. Choice (a) means the organization and gathering of people or equipment. Choice (b) means advancement. Choice (c) means an objective or a purpose.

51.   a   To *crave* means to desire, especially food. None of the other choices is a definition of the word *crave*. Choice (b) means to dislike greatly or to hate. Choice (c) means to avoid. Choice (d) means to cool.

52.   a   A *click* is a snap. All of the other choices refer to sounds also, but not to the sound of a *snap*. Choice (b) means the sound of something dropping into water. Choice (c) means the sound of a heavy object hitting a hard surface. Choice (d) means the sound of the letter "M" produced continuously and resonantly.

53.   a   A *guardian* is a person who is legally responsible for someone. All of the other choices also refer to relationships between people, but not to that of child and guardian. Choice (b) means a husband or wife. Choice (c) means an unmarried man. Choice (d) means an employee hired to perform domestic service, like a maid or a cook.

54.   c   *Temperate* means mild, especially in reference to climate. All of the other choices also refer to climate, but not to a mild one. Choice (a) means hot or humid. Choice (b) means extremely cold. Choice (d) means extremely dry.

55.   c   The *nobility* is the upper class. All of the other choices also refer to classes or groups of people, but not to the upper class. Choice (a) means the class composed of the armed forces. Choice (b) means the class composed of religious leaders. Choice (d) means the class composed of those in the teaching profession.

56.   b   *Distinguished* means respected. All of the other choices have some sounds like those in the word *distinguished*, but they have different meanings. Choice (a) means unhappy or frustrated. Choice (c) means depressed. Choice (d) means offended.

57.   d   *Unusually warm* means warmer than usual. Choice (a) means unusually cold. Choice (a) is the opposite of choice (d). Choices (b) and (c) are not definitions of the phrase *unusually warm*.

58.   a   *Aisles* are passageways between rows of seats. None of the other choices is a definition of the word *aisles*. Choice (b) means a structure spanning a body of water, a railroad, or another obstacle. Choice (c) means a smaller river that flows into a larger one. Choice (d) means a structure upon which or before which religious ceremonies may be celebrated.

59.   c   *Mutton* is meat from sheep. All of the other choices also refer to meat, but not to that of a sheep. Choice (a) means meat from pigs. Choice (b) means meat from calves. Choice (d) means meat from birds such as chickens, turkeys, ducks.

60.   a   An *alley* is a small street. All of the other choices also refer to small things, but not to streets. Choice (b) means a small cat. Choice (c) means a small coat. Choice (d) means a small house.

61.   c   *Initial* means first. Choice (b) means last. Choice (b) is the opposite of choice (c). The

other two choices are not definitions of the word *initial*. Choice (a) means common. Choice (d) means regular.

62. **d** *Next of kin* are family members. Only choice (d) is an idiomatic phrase. All of the other choices have some sounds like those in the word *kin*, but they have different meanings. *Kid* in choice (a) means a child or a baby goat. *Keg* in choice (b) means a small barrel. *King* in choice (c) means a monarch or a ruler.

63. **b** To *ponder* means to consider. All of the other choices have some sounds like those in the word *ponder*, but they have different meanings. Choice (a) means to travel without destination. Choice (c) means to move in a clumsy way. Choice (d) means to confuse.

64. **b** *Respectable* means deserving of respect. All of the other choices have some sounds like those in the word *respectable*, but they have different meanings. Choice (a) means having respect for others. Choice (c) means concerning. Choice (d) means particular ownership, especially in a sequence.

65. **d** *Recollection* is the ability to remember. All of the other choices have synonyms also. Choice (a) means communication. Choice (b) means forgetfulness. Choice (c) means flexibility.

66. **c** To *gnaw* means to bite. None of the other choices is a definition of the word *gnawing*. Choice (a) means discovering. Choice (b) means unearthing. Choice (d) means concealing.

67. **c** *Paralyzed* means unable to move. All of the other choices also refer to disabilities, but not to inability to move. Choice (a) means unable to see. Choice (b) means unable to hear. Choice (d) means unable to speak.

68. **b** A *tournament* is a competition, especially in sports. All of the other choices have some sounds like those in the word *tournament*, but they have different meanings. Choice (a) means a disagreement. Choice (c) means a sickness. Choice (d) means a penalty.

69. **b** *Hogs* are pigs. All of the other choices also refer to animals, but not to animals from which bacon, ham, and pork are cut. Choice (a) refers to chickens. Choice (c) refers to cows. Choice (d) refers to sheep.

70. **c** To *stack* means to pile. None of the other choices is a definition of the word *stack*. Choice (a) means to remove the cover or lid of something, or to expose. Choice (b) means to crease or to double. Choice (d) means to propel through the air or to hurl.

71. **b** A *warehouse* is a place where merchandise is stored. All of the other choices also refer to buildings or structures, but not to a storage area for chairs. Choice (a) means a small structure built to accommodate only one or two people, such as a telephone booth or a booth in a language laboratory. Choice (c) means a farm building to house animals and to store grain or farm machinery. Choice (d) means a structure to lift people and freight from one floor to another in a building.

72. **a** To *implore* means to beg. None of the other choices is a definition of the word *implore*. Choice (b) means to allow. Choice (c) means to assist. Choice (d) means to impose or to compel.

73. **b** To *dominate* means to rule. All of the other choices have some sounds like those in the word *dominate*, but they have different meanings. Choice (a) means to name, usually as a candidate. Choice (c) means to name, usually as an appointed official. Choice (d) means to attract or to charm.

74. **d** A *meteor* is a shooting star, a celestial body smaller than one mile in diameter. All of the other choices also refer to bodies in the universe, but not to shooting stars. Choice (a) means a man-made object or a moon that orbits a planet. The moon is a satellite of the earth. Choice (b) means a collection of stars, gas, and dust with a more-or-less definite shape. The Milky Way is the galaxy which contains the Earth. Choice (c) means a body larger than a meteor or a moon. Earth is the planet on which we live.

75. **b** *Braids* are interwoven strands, especially plaits of hair. All of the other choices have some sounds like those in the word *braids*, but they have different meanings. Choice (a) means intellectual capacity. Choice (c) means payment, usually for performing an illegal act. Choice (d) means women about to be married or recently married.

76. **b** *Odds* are probabilities. All of the other choices also refer to numbers, but not to probabilities. Choice (a) means the relative value of two quantities expressed as a quotient of one divided by the other. Choice (c) means the quotient of two quantities. Choice (d) means a fraction or ratio with 100 as the denominator. (½ is a ratio or a fraction. 50% is a percentage.)

77. **a** *Underground* means beneath the ground. None of the other choices is a definition of the word *underground*. Choice (b) means not to notice or to ignore. Choice (c) means earnings. Choice (d) means superior.

78. **b** *Harmless* means gentle or not dangerous. Choice (a) means harmful. Choice (a) is the opposite of choice (b). The other two choices are not definitions of the word *harmless*. Choice (c) means silent. Choice (d) means not well.

79. **b** An *opponent* is a rival. None of the other choices is a definition of the word *opponent*. Choice (a) means an argument. Choice (c) means a difference. Choice (d) means a feeling of resentment, usually one held over a long period of time.

80. **b** To *focus on* means to emphasize. None of the other choices is a definition of the phrase *focus on*. Choice (a) means not to notice or to overlook. Choice (c) means to clarify. Choice (d) means to comprehend.

81. **c** "Neither his [Sequoyah's] wife nor his friends offered him any encouragement . . ." (paragraph 1). Since Sequoyah had a wife, it must be concluded that he was married. Choice (a) is not mentioned, and may not be concluded from information in the passage. Choice (b) contradicts the fact that Sequoyah was a Cherokee Indian; Taskigi refers to the name of the village in which he was born. Choice (d) contradicts the fact that he worked twelve years to complete the alphabet with no encouragement from either his wife or friends.

82. **d** "As a result of a hunting accident that left him partially crippled, he enjoyed more leisure time than other tribesmen" (paragraph 1). Choice (a) refers to what Sequoyah did with his free time, not to the reason for his having free time. Choice (b) refers to what Sequoyah did before the accident that left him crippled. Choice (c) is not mentioned, and may not be concluded from information in the passage.

83. **c** "Alone in the woods, he spent hours playing with pieces of wood or making odd little marks on one stone with another . . . Sequoyah was obsessed with his dream of developing an alphabet . . ." (paragraph 1). Choice (a) contradicts the fact that his friends did not encourage him, from which it must be concluded that he did have friends. Choice (b) refers to the fact that he played with pieces of wood while he was experimenting with a system for an alphabet. Choice (d) refers to Sequoyah's activities as a hunter before he began spending so much time in the woods experimenting.

84. **b** "At first, Sequoyah tried to give every word a separate character, but eventually he . . . settled on assigning one character to each sound" (paragraph 2). Choice (a) refers to Sequoyah's first plan, not to the final alphabet. Choice (c) contradicts the fact that the alphabet could be learned in a few days. Choice (d) contradicts the fact that within a few months, the entire tribe was literate.

85. **c** "What he achieved twelve years later was a syllabary of eighty-six characters representing all of the sounds of Cherokee" (paragraph 2). Choice (a) refers to the length of time that it took for one person to learn the alphabet, not to the length of time that it took for Sequoyah to develop it. Choice (b) refers to the length of time that it took for the entire Cherokee nation to learn the alphabet. Choice (d) contradicts the fact that Sequoyah spent his earlier years as a hunter.

86. **c** "In this experiment, Robert Rosenthal and Lenore Jacobson investigated the way that innocent subjects might be affected by another person's [a teacher's] expectations" (sentence 1). Choice (a) refers to the tests used to measure the influence of teachers' expectations, not to the purpose of the investigation. Choice (b) contradicts the fact that the students were chosen for the experiment, not their teachers. Choice (d) contradicts the fact that teachers did not change the methods or materials used in teaching the designated students.

87. **b** ". . . they [Robert Rosenthal and Lenore Jacobson] selected students at random . . ." (sentence 3). Choices (a), (c), and (d) contradict the fact that students were selected at random, that is, by chance.

88. **d** "The experimenters concluded that they [the designated children] had performed better because they had been given more attention. Teachers had given them more positive reinforcement" (last two sentences). Choice (a) is not mentioned, and may not be concluded from information in the passage. Choice (b) contradicts the fact that the students were already in their regular classes prior to the experiment. Choice (c) contradicts the fact that the teachers did not change the methods or materials used in teaching the designated students.

89. **c** "Teachers had challenged them [the children] and had given them more positive reinforcement because they had expected more from them" (last sentence). Choice (a) is not mentioned, and may not be concluded from information in the passage. Choice (b) contradicts the fact that the teachers did not change their methods or materials. Choice (d) contradicts the fact that the teachers had challenged the children.

90. **c** "The experimenters concluded that they [the children] had performed better because . . . they [the teachers] had expected more from them" (last two sentences). Choices (a) and (d) are not mentioned, and may not be concluded from information in the passage. Choice (b) contradicts the fact that the teachers did not use different methods and materials for the designated children.

91. **b** ". . . During the next decade [the 1970s], every one of the dozens of science fiction movies released was compared to *2001* and . . . found sadly lacking" (paragraph 1). Choice (a) contradicts the fact that other movies were compared to *2001* and found lacking. Choices (c) and (d) contradict the fact that *Star Wars* was reminiscent of the artistic standards set by *2001*. The other science fiction movies were described as having repetitive plots.

92. **c** "After *2001*, the dominant theme of science fiction films shifted from the adventures of space travel to the problems created on earth by man's mismanagement of the natural environment . . ." (paragraph 3). Choices (a), (b), and (d) refer to the themes of *2001* and *Star Wars*, not to the themes of the majority of science fiction films made between 1970 and 1977.

93.   **d**   "In my opinion, until *Star Wars* was released in 1977, science fiction films were reduced to shallow symbolism disguising to a greater or lesser degree a series of repetitive plots" (paragraph 4). Choice (a) refers to a movie made in 1968, not in the 1970s. Choices (b) and (c) refer to two of the twenty-nine films that were described as shallow and repetitive.

94.   **b**   ". . . in my opinion, much of the movie's power [that of *2001*] was achieved through . . . the musical score. . . Spectacular camera work was edited to correspond precisely to the ebb and flow of the music" (paragraph 2). Choice (a) contradicts the fact that, in the author's opinion, much of *2001*'s power and appeal was achieved through relatively inexpensive means. Choice (c) refers to the twenty-nine films made between 1970 and 1977, not to *2001*. Choice (d) was not mentioned in reference to *2001*. Shallow symbolism was mentioned in reference to science fiction films made between 1970 and 1977.

95.   **c**   ". . . science fiction films were reduced to shallow symbolism disguising . . . a series of repetitive plots" (paragraph 4). Choices (a), (b), and (d) are not mentioned in reference to films of the 1970s. Camera work, music, and special effects were all mentioned as being very good in *2001*.

96.   **b**   "In time, the migration became a habit, and now, although the glaciers have disappeared, the habit continues" (paragraph 1). Choice (a) contradicts the fact that the habit of migration continues. Choice (c) contradicts the fact that the migration had not stopped, and, thus, could not begin again. Choice (d) is not mentioned, and may not be concluded from information in the passage.

97.   **b**   "When the [tropical] region became overpopulated, many species were crowded north. During the summer, there was plenty of food, but during the winter, scarcity forced them to return to the tropics" (paragraph 2). Choices (a) and (c) refer to the area north of the tropics, not to the tropics. Choice (d) is not mentioned in reference to the tropics, and may not be concluded from information in the passage.

98.   **b**   "One scientist has been able to cause midwinter migrations by exposing birds to artificial periods of daylight" (paragraph 3). Choices (a), (c), and (d) are not mentioned, and may not be concluded from information in the passage. Although the stimulation of certain glands in the birds' bodies may be caused by increasing daylight, the purpose of the experiment was to draw conclusions about migration.

99.   **b**   Photoperiodism "suggests a relationship between increasing daylight and the stimulation of certain glands in the birds' bodies that may prepare them for migration" (paragraph 3). Choice (a) refers to an experiment in which exposure to artificial daylight caused birds to migrate, not to the theory of photoperiodism. Choice (c) contradicts the fact that a scientist was able to cause migration by exposing birds to artificial periods of daylight. Choice (d) is not mentioned, and may not be concluded from information in this passage.

100.   **a**   "Although no one is certain why migration occurs, there are several theories" (paragraph 1). Choice (b) is not mentioned, and may not be concluded from information in the passage. Choices (c) and (d) are both theories of migration that are explained in the passage, but the author does not support either one of them.

Model Test Three

Answer Key

1.	a	21.	d	41.	b	61.	a	81.	c
2.	b	22.	a	42.	d	62.	c	82.	d
3.	a	23.	d	43.	a	63.	c	83.	b
4.	b	24.	d	44.	a	64.	c	84.	c
5.	c	25.	c	45.	b	65.	a	85.	d
6.	d	26.	a	46.	d	66.	d	86.	c
7.	b	27.	d	47.	a	67.	c	87.	d
8.	d	28.	b	48.	c	68.	c	88.	d
9.	a	29.	a	49.	c	69.	c	89.	c
10.	c	30.	a	50.	a	70.	a	90.	b
11.	b	31.	b	51.	b	71.	d	91.	b
12.	d	32.	a	52.	d	72.	c	92.	b
13.	a	33.	a	53.	b	73.	b	93.	c
14.	c	34.	b	54.	b	74.	c	94.	c
15.	a	35.	c	55.	b	75.	b	95.	c
16.	c	36.	c	56.	c	76.	a	96.	c
17.	a	37.	b	57.	d	77.	b	97.	b
18.	b	38.	c	58.	b	78.	b	98.	c
19.	b	39.	c	59.	c	79.	a	99.	c
20.	a	40.	c	60.	c	80.	b	100.	b

Explanatory Answers

1. **a** An imperative verb form must be used to express a request.

2. **b** An *-ing* verb form must be used to express a compound noun. Remember, the *-ing* form specifies the activity; a *sewing machine* is a machine that assists you *to sew*.

3. **a** *However* must be used at the end of a clause to express contrast. *Although* he plays well, "he *still* plays well," and "*but* he plays well" would also be correct.

4. **b** An *-ing* verb must be used after *be used to* to express custom. Remember, with the verb *is*, the custom exists at the present time. "*She used to be* told" would be correct if the custom existed in the past.

5. **c** *In spite of* must be used before a noun phrase that does not have a verb. "He's going to play *even though he is* injured" and "he's going to play *although he is* injured" would also be correct.

6. **a** *Have* and a participle must be used after *would rather* to express preference in the past.

7. **b** *Still* must be used between the subject and verb to express a continued situation. Remember, *still* means *continued*; *already* means *previously*.

8. **d** The adverb *besides* must be used to express addition. Remember, one of the meanings of *besides* is *in addition to*.

9. **a** A verb word (simple verb) must be used in the clause after the verb *to suggest*.

10. **c** An *-ing* verb form must be used after *will have been* to express projected future action.

11. **b** *Otherwise* must be used to express a condition. Remember, *otherwise* means *if not*.

12. **d** *Could*, a subject, and *have*, in that order, must be used in a question.

13. **a** The conjunction *but* must be used to express an exception. Remember, one of the meanings of *but* is *except*.

14. **c** *Have been* must be used to express a continuous activity. Remember, *for* or *since* is usually used with continuous activity.

15. **a** *Had* and a participle must be used after the verb *wish* to express a past desire.

16. **c** *The* must be used with an *-est* form to compare three or more things.

17. **a** *So much so* must be used to express a degree. Remember, *so much so* means *to the extent*.

18. **b** An infinitive must be used after the verb phrase *to be left*.

19. **b** An *-ing* verb form or a noun phrase must be used after *because of*. A possessive pronoun such as *her* must be used with an *-ing* form.

20. **a** An infinitive must be used after the imperative phrase *be sure*.

21. **d** The preposition *of* must be used after the verb *to think*. An *-ing* verb form must be used after the preposition.

22. **a** An auxiliary, subject, and main verb, in that order, must be used after an initial negative like *never again*.

23. **d** An adjective must be used to modify the subject *we*. Choice (b) is a noun. Choice (c) is a verb. Choice (a) is an adjective, but it would refer to the *gas mileage*, not to *us*. Remember, an *-ed* adjective is used to express an effect; an *-ing* adjective is used to express a cause.

24. **d** *Would have* and a participle must be used before a clause with *if*, and *had*, and a participle, to express a condition.

25. **c** *Whoever* must be used as a subject. Remember, *whoever* means *any person who*.

26. **a** *Should* must be used to express a condition. "*If* he *changes* his mind" would also be correct.

27. **d** An adverb must be used to modify the verb *to speak*. "He speaks *faster*" would also be correct.

28. **b** The adjective *worth* must be used after a stated or implied verb to express value. Remember, *worth* means *equal to*.

29. **a** A subject and verb, in that order, must be used in the clause after a question word.

30. **a** The preposition *for* must be used after the verb phrase *thank you*.

31. **b** The relative pronoun *that* must be used in a clause in which full information is given. "The city . . . was Miami."

32. **a** Adjectives of number, size, and color must be used in that order.

33. **a** A verb word (simple verb) must be used after *let's*. An *-ing* verb form must be used after the verb word *be*.

34. **b** The adjective phrase *a little* must be used to refer to the non-count noun *money*.

35. **c** *For* must be used with an adverbial phrase to express duration of time. "I haven't gotten a letter *since* a long time *ago*" would also be correct.

36. **c** An *-ing* verb form or a noun phrase must be used after *how about*.

37. **b** An *-ing* verb form must be used after the verb *to consider*.

38. **c** *Of all* must be used to express selection. Remember, *of all* means *from among all*.

39. **c** An infinitive must be used after the verb *to hope*.

40. **c** *Have* must be used with *got to* to express necessity. Remember, *have got to* means *must*. "We *must* talk to the director" would also be correct.

41. **b** *Elevation* means altitude. All of the other choices have some sounds like those in the word *elevation,* but they have different meanings. Choice (a) means gradual change, usually from simple to complex. Choice (c) means review or appraisal. Choice (d) means detailed information.

42. **d** *Tenants* are occupants, especially of a rented house or apartment. All of the other choices refer to relationships, but not to that between a landlord and tenant. Choice (a) means a husband or wife. Choice (b) means a person under a doctor's care. Choice (c) means a person who buys goods or services.

43. **a** A *procedure* means a method. All of the other choices may describe some of the requirements of a registration procedure, but they do not define the word *procedure*. Choice (b) means a person with authority. Choice (c) means a given day, month, and year. Choice (d) means income or compensation.

44. **a** To *subdue* means to defeat or to quiet. None of the other choices is a definition of the word *subdue*. Choice (b) means to help. Choice (c) means to examine. Choice (d) means to begin.

45. **b** A *choir* is a group of singers. All of the other choices have some sounds like those in the word *choir,* but they have different meanings. Choice (a) means a routine task. Choice (c) means a center. Choice (d) means joy or happiness.

46. **d** *Annual* means yearly. All of the other choices also have one-word synonyms, although they are words which are not used very often. The synonym for choice (a) would be *diurnal;* for choice (b), *hebdomadal;* for choice (c), *menstrual*.

47. **a** *Manuscripts* are unpublished documents, especially books. All of the other choices also refer to books or documents, but not to documents that would be read by an editor. Choice (b) means a dedication. Choice (c) means a set of sacred or authoritative writings. Choice (d) means people who receive a newspaper or magazine.

48. **c** To *tackle* means to throw down. All of the other choices have some sounds like those in the word *tackle,* but they have different meanings. Choice (a) means to tease or to cause laughter. Choice (b) means to drip. Choice (d) means to shine on and off.

49. **c** *Quaint* means curious, colorful, and old-fashioned. All of the other choices may describe the quaint Amish communities, but they do not define the word *quaint*. Choice (a) means calm. Choice (b) means rustic or agricultural. Choice (d) means little.

50. **a** A *confession* is an admission of guilt. All of the other choices have some sounds like

those in the word *confession,* but they have different meanings. Choice (b) means disorganization. Choice (c) means a compromise. Choice (d) means informal talk.

51. **b**   *Hurried* means rapid or hasty. None of the other choices is a definition of the word *hurried.* Choice (a) means not difficult. Choice (c) means content or cheerful. Choice (d) means secure or protected.

52. **d**   *Barely* means just or scarcely. All of the other choices refer to frequency, not to sufficiency. Choice (a) means at every time. Choice (b) means few times. Choice (c) means not at all.

53. **b**   *Wedges* are triangular shapes. All of the other choices also refer to shapes, but not to triangular ones. Choice (a) means a square shape. Choice (c) means a round shape. Choice (d) means a mound-like, pointed shape.

54. **b**   To *authorize* means to permit. Choice (d) means to prohibit. Choice (d) is the opposite of choice (b). The other two choices are not definitions of the word *authorize.* Choice (a) means to assist. Choice (c) means to insist or to compel.

55. **b**   *Haughty* means proud. None of the other choices is a definition of the word *haughty.* Choice (a) means sad. Choice (c) means envious. Choice (d) means stubborn.

56. **c**   A *dean* is a university administrator above a director and below a vice president. All of the other choices are university personnel, but not personnel between a director and a vice president in importance. Choice (a) means a clerical or secretarial staff member. Choice (b) means a teacher whose rank is above that of both an assistant and an associate professor. Choice (d) means a teacher whose rank is above that of a lecturer and below that of an assistant professor.

57. **d**   *Indifference* is disinterest. All of the other choices also refer to negative responses, but not to a lack of interest. Choice (a) means lack of organization. Choice (b) means lack of satisfaction, especially in response to an expectation. Choice (c) means lack of agreement.

58. **b**   *Patiently* means in a quiet, calm manner. The phrases in choices (a), (c), and (d) may describe a person waiting patiently in line, but they do not define the word *patiently.*

59. **c**   *Herbs* are plants, usually with medicinal properties. All of the other choices refer to treatments for illness, but they do not define the word *herbs.* Choice (a) means a regulated selection of food, usually given to help in weight loss. Choice (b) means physical or mental activity. Choice (d) means medicine.

60. **c**   A *grudge* is a feeling of resentment, usually one held over a long period of time. None of the other choices is a definition of the word *grudge.* Choice (a) means to express discontentment or to mutter. Choice (b) means a sharp reply. Choice (d) means an error.

61. **a**   *Spacious* means large. All of the other choices may describe a spacious apartment, but they do not define the word *spacious.* Choice (b) means attractive or pretty. Choice (c) means costly. Choice (d) means content.

62. **c**   To *overflow* means to flood. All of the other choices have some sounds like those in the word *overflow,* but they have different meanings. Choice (a) means to defeat. Choice (b) means to catch up with or surpass. Choice (d) means to supervise.

63. **c**   To *compete* means to take part in a contest. All of the other choices have some sounds like those in the word *compete,* but they have different meanings. Choice (a) means to express dissatisfaction. Choice (b) means to force. Choice (d) means to create, especially music.

64. **c** To *spin* means to turn. All of the other choices have some sounds like those in the word *spinning*, but they have different meanings. Choice (a) means increasing in size. Choice (b) means decreasing in size. Choice (b) is the opposite of choice (a). Choice (d) means increasing in rate or velocity, or accelerating.

65. **a** To *confide* means to trust. Choice (b) means to doubt. Choice (c) means to share an opinion or to concur. Choice (d) means to hold a different opinion or to conflict. Choice (b) is the opposite of choice (a); choice (d) is the opposite of choice (c).

66. **d** *Delivery* service is a service whereby purchases are brought to the buyer, usually at his or her home. All of the other choices have some sounds like those in the word *delivery*, but they have different meanings. Choice (a) means a short wait. Choice (b) means an exhibit. Choice (c) means dark or gloomy.

67. **c** *Toads* are amphibians, related to and resembling frogs. All of the other choices are animals also, but they do not look like frogs. Choice (a) means an animal which may look like a rat. Choice (b) means an animal which may look like a cat. Choice (d) means an animal which may look like a monkey.

68. **c** To *stimulate* means to cause. None of the other choices is a definition of the word *stimulate*. Choice (a) means to review or to examine. Choice (b) means to discover. Choice (d) means to alter.

69. **c** *Suspicious* means questionable; it describes behavior that inspires mistrust. All of the other choices have some sounds like those in the word *suspicious*, but they have different meanings. Choice (a) means aggressive or aspiring. Choice (b) means sociable or talkative. Choice (d) means well known or famous, usually for unfavorable reasons.

70. **a** *Adequate* means satisfactory. All of the other choices may describe what would be necessary for housing to be adequate in a certain situation, but they do not define the word *adequate*. Choice (b) means beautiful. Choice (c) means extra. Choice (d) means inexpensive.

71. **d** *Neutral* means fair or unbiased. Choice (b) means unfair. Choice (b) is the opposite of choice (d). The other two choices are not definitions of the word *neutral*. Choice (a) means unusual or rare. Choice (c) means not permanent.

72. **c** *Scope* is the range of one's plans or activities. None of the other choices is a definition of the word *scope*. Choice (a) means a large, flat dish used for carrying things. Choice (b) means a border. Choice (d) means a yard, usually one planted with grass.

73. **b** *Skillful* means able. All of the other choices may describe a skillful surgeon, but they do not define the word *skillful*. Choice (a) means well-known. Choice (c) means occupied. Choice (d) means unusual or exceptional.

74. **c** *Logical* means reasonable or consistent with earlier statements or events. All of the other choices have some sounds like those in the word *logical*, but they have different meanings. Choice (a) means supernatural. Choice (b) means funny or amusing. Choice (d) means governmental or bureaucratic.

75. **b** *Vibration* means movement back and forth. All of the other choices describe what may accompany or cause vibration, but they do not define the word *vibration*. Choice (a) means confused sound, usually loud. Choice (c) means velocity. Choice (d) means degree of heat or cold.

76. **a** A *lull* is a pause, especially a short period of quiet. All of the other choices refer to pauses, but not to a short period of quiet. Choice (b) means a pause between acts in a play or selections in a concert. Choice (c) means a pause in the school day to give

children time to play. Choice (d) means a pause in work, usually as a protest against low salaries or poor working conditions.

77. **b** *Minimum* means least. Choice (c) means maximum. Choice (c) is the opposite of choice (b). The other two choices are not definitions of the word *minimum*. Choice (a) means the highest quality. Choice (d) means initial.

78. **b** To *ruffle* means to upset. All of the other choices also have synonyms. The synonym of choice (a) would be to exhaust; of choice (c), to cheer; and of choice (d), to frighten.

79. **a** *Cordial* means friendly. None of the other choices is a definition of the word *cordial*. Choice (b) means reserved. Choice (c) means unpretentious. Choice (d) means influenced.

80. **b** *Accuracy* means exactness or correctness. None of the other choices is a definition of the word *accuracy*. Choice (a) means attention. Choice (c) means system or repetition. Choice (d) means a shared opinion or a concurrence.

81. **c** ". . . the original is coated with silver to conduct electricity, and then electroplated with nickel" (paragraph 2). The use described in choice (a) is not mentioned, and may not be concluded from information in the passage. Choice (b) refers to the purpose of the sapphire or ruby stylus, not to the purpose of the silver. Choice (d) refers to the purpose of the mother matrix.

82. **d** ". . . the master matrix is electroplated with nickel to produce a positive . . . called a mother matrix" (paragraph 3). Choice (a) refers to the master matrix, not to the mother matrix. Choice (b) refers to the negatives produced by the mother matrix, not to the mother matrix itself. Choice (c) refers to the flat aluminum disc from which the master matrix is made.

83. **b** ". . . a stylus cuts a continuous groove in the lacquer coating" (paragraph 1). Choice (a) refers to a property of silver, not of lacquer. Choice (c) refers to the hydraulic press. Choice (d) is not mentioned as a property of lacquer, and may not be concluded from information in the passage.

84. **c** "A preform of shellac compound or plastic is placed between the stampers" (paragraph 4). Choice (a) refers to the metals used in electroplating, not to those used in making preforms. Choice (b) refers to the gems used in making a stylus. Choice (d) refers to the materials used in making an original record.

85. **d** "When an impression of the stampers has been made in the material, the press is quickly cooled and opened. The grooves in the record correspond to those in the original lacquer disc" (paragraph 4). There are several steps in the production of a commercial record, but only the last step is that from which a record is directly made. Choice (a) refers to the step from which a master matrix is made. Choice (b) refers to the step from which a mother matrix is made. Choice (c) refers to the step from which a stamper is made.

86. **c** "Wild Bill Hickok was elected sheriff. . ." (paragraph 1). Although Hickok was fond of elegantly tailored European clothes, Choices (a) and (b) are not mentioned as either the national origin or the occupation of Hickok. Choice (d) refers to the men Hickok pursued in his duties as sheriff.

87. **d** "But his [Hickok's] most striking feature was his yellow hair" (paragraph 2). Choices (a) and (c) are mentioned as features of Hickok, but neither is referred to as his most striking or distinguished feature. Although Hickok shot holes in a hat during a bet, choice (b) is not mentioned as a feature of Hickok.

88. **d** "While most of his fellow lawmen favored informal clothes, Bill was a notorious

dandy" (paragraph 2). Since Hickok had a reputation as one of the best gunmen and most colorful characters in all of the territory, it may be concluded that he was famous, as stated in choice (a). Since he wore elegantly tailored suits, it may be concluded that he was elegant, as stated in choice (b). Since he bragged that he could shoot more than one hole in a hat that had been thrown in the air, it may be concluded that he was boastful, as stated in choice (c).

89. c ". . . he sported a knife that he tied around his waist in a bright red sash" (paragraph 2). Choices (a) and (d) refer to where he carried his guns, not his knife. Choice (b) is not mentioned, and may not be concluded from information in the passage.

90. b ". . . after bragging that he could shoot more than one hole in a hat that had been thrown in the air, he shot a row of evenly-spaced holes along the edge of the brim. . ." Choice (a) refers to a different story about Hickok. Choice (c) contradicts the fact that the hat was thrown in the air. Choice (d) is not mentioned, and may not be concluded from information in the passage.

91. b "One reason that the cost [of health care] is so high can be traced to advances in medical technology that include expensive equipment. . ." (paragraph 2). Choices (a) and (c) contradict the fact that the high cost can be traced to technological advances. Choice (d) contradicts the fact that expensive equipment requires highly-trained, highly-paid personnel to run it.

92. b "By 1980, the same hospital was charging $200" (paragraph 1). Choice (a) refers to the cost of one night in a hospital in 1970, not 1980. Choice (c) refers to the cost of intensive care, not one night in a regular hospital room. Choice (d) refers to the cost of an anesthesiologist.

93. c "The cost of health care in the United States has . . . tripled during the last ten years . . ." (paragraph 1). The number in choice (a) refers to the number of years during which costs have increased ten times, not to the increase itself. Choice (b) refers to the increase during the past twenty-five, not the past ten years. Choice (d) is not mentioned, and may not be concluded from information in the passage.

94. c "As an example [of advances in medical technology], the CAT, a computerized scanner used for diagnostic purposes, now costs $600,000" (paragraph 2). Choices (a) and (b) are both mentioned in the passage, but not in reference to the CAT. Choice (d) refers to the highly-trained personnel needed to run the CAT, not to the equipment itself.

95. c ". . . unlike many other countries, the U.S. does not have a national health insurance plan" (paragraph 3). Choices (a) and (b) are not mentioned, and may not be concluded from information in the passage. Choice (d) contradicts the fact that the CAT computerized scanner is mentioned as an example of the expensive equipment that has caused hospital costs to go up in the U.S.

96. c ". . . you will see the shining dome of the State Capitol Building, made of twenty-four-karat gold" (paragraph 2). Choices (a) and (b) refer to the skyscrapers, not to the Capitol Building. Choice (d) refers to the office buildings.

97. b "The tallest building in the skyline, the First National Bank Building, is surrounded by other giants . . ." (paragraph 1). Choice (a) refers to the building from which the view can be seen, not to the tallest building. Choice (c) refers to one of the giant skyscrapers surrounding the tallest building. Choice (d) refers to the building with the gold dome.

98. c ". . . Peachtree Center [is] a complex that contains the largest merchandise mart in the South" (paragraph 1). Choice (a) is the second busiest airport in the country, not

the location of the largest merchandise mart. Choice (b) is the largest fresh fruit and vegetable center in the South. Choice (d) is the famous hotel from which the view can be seen.

99. **c** ". . . the South Expressway leading to Hartsfield-Atlanta International Airport . . ." (paragraph 1). Choices (a) and (b) refer to the structures that can be seen in the distance, not to the structure to which the South Expressway leads. Choice (d) refers to a structure in the foreground.

100. **b** ". . . you will see a dramatic view of this beautiful city . . ." (paragraph 1). Choice (a) contradicts the fact that the author believes the city is beautiful. The opinions in choices (c) and (d) are not mentioned, and may not be concluded from information in the passage.

Continued Study for Grammar, Vocabulary, and Reading Comprehension

CHAPTER 5

Continued Study for Grammar, Vocabulary, and Reading Comprehension

A THREE-STEP STUDY PROGRAM

Because the Michigan Test of English Language Proficiency has three parts, you must develop your knowledge in three different language skills. Then you must apply your knowledge and skills to the test.

You can do this by following three steps:

1. **Study one or more good grammar textbooks** and **one or more advanced-level reading textbooks** to review your knowledge of structures, reading skills and vocabulary.
2. **Practice answering problems with specific structures and reading for vocabulary and comprehension** to improve your skills in grammar, vocabulary, and reading.
3. **Apply your knowledge and skills to the test.**

Step One: Study One or More Good Grammar Textbooks and One or More Advanced-Level Reading Textbooks.

There are many good grammar books. Some of the most complete ones are listed for you on pages 158-159.

There are also many good reading books. If you are enrolled in an English program, you probably have a good reading book. *Attend your reading class every day*. The best preparation for the Michigan Test of English Language Proficiency is daily practice in grammar, vocabulary, and reading.

If you are not enrolled in an English program, buy a good advanced-level reading book or borrow one from the library. There are dozens of good books. Some of them are listed below:

Baudoin, E. Margaret, et al. *Reader's Choice*. Ann Arbor, Michigan: University of Michigan Press, 1977.

Harris, David P. *Reading Improvement Exercises for Students of English as a Second Language*. Englewood Cliffs, New Jersey: Prentice-Hall, 1966.

Hirasawa, Louise, and Markstein, Linda. *Developing Reading Skills*. Rowley, Massachusetts: Newbury House, 1974.

Sharpe, Pamela J. *Barron's How to Prepare for the TOEFL (Test of English as a Foreign Language)*. Woodbury, N.Y.: Barron's Educational Series, Inc., 1977.

Sharpe, Pamela J. *Barron's Practice Exercises for the TOEFL (Test of English as a Foreign Language)*. Woodbury, N.Y.: Barron's Educational Series, Inc., 1980.

Turner, David R. *Scoring High on Reading Tests*. New York: Arco, 1978.

Step Two: Practice Answering Problems with Specific Structures and Practice Reading for Vocabulary and Comprehension

There are six classes of structures that you should review. They are listed below, with examples from the model tests in this book.

Specific Structures

1. VERB STRUCTURES

More than half of the grammar questions will be problems with verbs. It will be helpful to review all verbal structures, especially:

imperatives
verbs that require *-ing* complements
verbs that require infinitive complements
semi-modals
modals
have and a participle
let and *wish*
special verbs that require simple form complements
conditionals
idioms with *get*
verbs that require prepositions
passives

Example of Imperatives

"May I take a message?"
"Yes, please *have* him call me when he gets back to the office."

Example of Verbs that Require *-ing* Complements

"How do you know that they were discussing your family?"
"Because they *stopped talking* when I entered the room."

Example of Verbs that Require Infinitive Complements

"There are two Olympic medalists entered in the competition."
"How could Mike ever *hope to win?*"

Example of Semi-Modals

"I always get confused about tipping in this country."
"Usually you *ought to* leave 15 percent for a waiter or waitress."

Example of Modals (Present, Future Time)

"Do you believe that James will apologize to Mary?"
"I don't know. He *should*."

Example of Modals (Past Time)

"*Might you have* left your purse in the car?"
"No. I'm sure that I had it with me in the restaurant."

Example of *have* and a participle with *since*

"I didn't know that Carol was a waitress here."
"She *has been working* here on Saturdays *since* June."

Examples of *let* and *let's*

"What did your parents think about your decision?"
"They always *let* me *do* what I think I should."

"Mother will probably be tired when she gets home."
"I know. *Let's be* preparing dinner when she gets home."

Example of *wish*

"Are you afraid to drive home?"
"Yes. I *wish* it *would* stop snowing."

Examples of Special Verbs that Require Verb Form Complements (*Insist, Suggest*)

"I think that the Smiths were embarrassed by Jane's generosity."
"She *insisted that they accept* it as a gift."

"Did Kathy have any ideas for Jim?"
"She *suggested that he send* a card with all of our names on it."

Example of Conditionals

"Your pictures are beautiful!"
"We *would have taken* more if we *hadn't run out* of film."

Examples of Idioms with *get*

"Are you busy?"
"We're just *getting ready* to go out."

"You've been sick quite a few times since you arrived."
"I just can't *get used to* the cold weather."

Examples of Verbs that Require Prepositions

"Who won the Superbowl football game?"
"Houston. Haven't you been *listening to* the news?"

"What's bothering you, Kathy?"
"I'm *worried about* taking my oral exams for my Ph.D."

Example of Passives

"Didn't you forget to count your living expenses when you wrote up this budget?"
"No. That *has been taken* into consideration."

2. ADJECTIVE STRUCTURES

Adjective structures should be reviewed, especially *-ed* and *-ing* adjectives, quantity expressions, and classification expressions.

Examples of *-ed* and *-ing* Adjectives

"How was the *movie?*"
"To tell the truth, it was rather *disappointing.*"

"Did you enjoy your guests?"
"Yes. Their *children* are so well *mannered* that I always enjoy having them visit me."

Example of Quantity Expressions

"Are you ready to leave?"
"I have *a little money*, but I should probably cash a check first."

Example of Classification Expressions

"Why are you staring?"
"I've never seen *that kind of tree* before."

3. COMPARATIVE STRUCTURES

Comparative structures should be reviewed.

Examples of Comparisons

"Do you know Mr. Brown?"
"Yes. There's no one more generous *than* he is."

"Did you like the book that I gave you?"
"*Of all* the novels that I've read, I enjoyed this one *the most*."

"Did you like my girl friend?"
"Very much. She's *as* charming *as* you said she was."

"Which woman are you going to vote for?" *[two candidates]*
"I'm not sure. Everyone says that Joan is *smarter*."

"That's a nice bike."
"We bought *the cheapest one* we could find because we don't plan to use it very much."

4. PRONOUN STRUCTURES

Pronoun structures should be reviewed, especially relative pronouns.

Examples of Relative Pronouns

"I wish you would just forget about it."
"I can't. I want to know *what* she said about us."

"Which city did you like most?"
"I enjoyed all of the cities on the tour, but the city *that* I most enjoyed was Miami, Florida."

Examples of Other Pronouns

"Whose luggage is this?"
"I believe it's *his*."

"Who is responsible for this?"
"*Whoever* did it, I hope that the police find him."

5. CONNECTIVE WORDS

Connective words should be reviewed, especially adverbs, conjunctions, and prepositions.

Examples of Adverbs

"What did he do?"
"He ran a red light; *moreover,* when the police officer stopped him, he refused to take the sobriety test."

"What do you do when you get a headache?"
"Since I'm allergic to aspirin, I take Tylenol *instead*."

"What do you want to do?"
"Let's try to convince everyone to agree tonight; *otherwise,* we'll have to have another meeting."

"Steve never practices the piano anymore."
"He plays very well, *however*."

"Does your telephone work now?"
"No. It *still* needs to be fixed."

Examples of Conjunctions

"My watch started up again."
"You should take it to be repaired *even though* it's working now."

"They don't have much in their apartment yet."
"*Since* they're planning to live here only until Bob gets his degree, they don't want to buy much furniture."

Examples of Prepositions

"I'd like to go, but I have a date on Saturday."
"That's okay. If we leave today, we can probably be back *by* the weekend."

"Do you have any more of these briefcases?"
"I'm sorry. We've sold all *but* this one."

6. WORD ORDER

Word order should be reviewed, especially negative introductions, question word clauses, and adjectives in sequence.

Example of Negative Introductions

"Mary said that you locked your keys in your car last night and had to walk home."
"*Never have I been* so embarrassed!"

Example of Question Word Clauses

"Someone was waiting for you in your office, but he's gone now."
"Don't you know *who it was?*"

Example of Adjectives in Sequence

"Do you have any pets?"
"Yes, I have *two small black* kittens."

Step Three: Apply Your Knowledge and Skill to the Test

To apply your knowledge and skill means to use information that you have already studied to help you in a new situation.

Part I—Grammar

On Part I of the Michigan Test of English Language Proficiency, you won't see exactly the same questions that you have studied in your textbooks. But you will see questions about the specific structures that you have reviewed in Step Two. And the specific structures are explained in your textbooks. If you understand the specific structures in your textbooks, you should understand the questions on Part I of your test.

First, memorize the generalizations in your textbooks. Remember, generalizations are often printed in boxes or set apart with a title. They are the most important things to study in your textbooks.

Now learn to recognize the information from your textbooks as it appears on the test.

TEXTBOOK FORMAT

The exercises below are like the exercises in your textbooks. They are printed in textbook format.

1. John is *interested* in art.

2. Mr. Brown said that he was more than satisfied with Miss Taylor's work; _moreover_, he gave her a $500 raise.

3. I _haved lived_ around here since I was a child.

4. New York is larger _than_ Washington.

5. Is Macy's the store _that_ employs the most people?

6. I wish that I _had received_ this letter before the office closed for the day.

7. Since they aren't answering their telephone, they _must have left_.

8. They finished _building_ the house yesterday.

9. He would probably find a job if he _got_ a haircut.

10. Ask the clerk _how much it costs_.

TEST FORMAT

The exercises below are the same exercises. But they are printed in test format.

1. "Why is John taking this class?"
   "John is _____ in art."

   a. interest
   b. interesting
   c. interested
   d. interests

2. "What did her boss say?"
   "Mr. Brown said that he was more than satisfied with Miss Taylor's work; _____ he gave her a $50 raise."

   a. moreover
   b. although
   c. despite
   d. however

3. "When did you move to Miami?"
   "I _____ around here since I was a child."

   a. lived
   b. have lived
   c. am living
   d. was living

4. "Washington is the biggest city that I have ever seen!"
   "New York is larger _____ Washington."

   a. to
   b. than
   c. that
   d. as

5. "Is Macy's the store _____ employs the most people?"
"Yes, it is."

   a. that
   b. what
   c. where
   d. it

6. "It's too late to call them, isn't it?"
"Yes. I wish that I _____ this letter before the office closed for the day."

   a. received
   b. have received
   c. had received
   d. would received

7. "Do you think that they are on their way here?"
"Yes. Since they aren't answering their telephone, they _____."

   a. must leave
   b. must left
   c. must be leave
   d. must have left

8. "Everything looks like new."
"They finished _____ the house yesterday."

   a. to build
   b. building
   c. build
   d. the build

9. "What's the problem? Bill seems very qualified to me."
"He is. And would probably find a job if he _____ a haircut."

   a. got
   b. gets
   c. had got
   d. has

10. "There isn't any price on this."
"As the clerk _____. He just put them on sale."

   a. how much costs it
   b. it costs how much
   c. how it costs much
   d. how much it costs

Can you recognize the information from your textbooks when it is printed in *test format?*

If you can *learn the generalizations* from your textbooks and *recognize the information* when it is printed in test format, you are ready to take Part I of the Michigan Test of English Language Proficiency. You can apply your knowledge and skill to the test.

Answer Key

1.	c	6.	c
2.	a	7.	d
3.	b	8.	b
4.	b	9.	a
5.	a	10.	d

Part II—Vocabulary

On Part II of the Michigan Test of English Language Proficiency, you won't see exactly the same questions that you have studied in your textbooks. But you will see questions about vocabulary that you have learned from your textbooks. If you understand the vocabulary in your textbooks, you should understand most of the words on Part II of your test.

First, learn new vocabulary in context in your textbooks. When you see new words, try to guess their meaning by reading them in the context of a sentence or paragraph. Use your dictionary to check your guesses.

Because there are so many words to learn, it is a good idea to put a mark by each word that you have looked up in your dictionary. If you have to look up the same word more than once, you will see the mark. You will know that it is a good word to learn.

Now learn to recognize information from your textbooks as it appears on the test.

TEXTBOOK FORMAT

The exercises below are like the exercises in your textbooks. They are printed in textbook format.

1. Write a synonym or a definition of the word underlined in the sentence.

   Most people are <u>flattered</u> when we ask their opinions.

   Flattered means happy or pleased.

2. Underline the word that has the same meaning as the first word.

   AMUSING *funny* serious   true   strange

3. Match the word in the left column with the correct meaning in the right column.

c	sympathetic	a.	causing worry
b	humorous	b.	causing laughter
a	disturbing	c.	causing pity
d	dreadful	d.	causing fear

4. Fill in the blank space with a word that makes sense in the context of the sentence.

   When you have a health problem you should ____*consult*____ a doctor.

5. Fill in the blank space with a word that has the same meaning as *force*, *danger*, or *disorder*.

   There seems to be a great deal of ___*violence*___ on television.

6. Use the definitions listed to help you read this passage.

   Some of the symptoms[1] were difficult to understand. Every day they seemed to vary.[2] And his condition continued to deteriorate.[3]

   _____

   [1]**symptoms** signs of disease
   [2]**vary** to change
   [3]**deteriorate** to get worse

7. Study the word in the box. Look it up in your dictionary.
   Write the definitions in the space provided.

   One-celled forms of marine animals may have been the first signs of life on this planet.
   _*marine – sea; water*_____

8. Study the words listed before you read this passage.
   arose past tense of *arise*; to go up
   throng crowd

   When the Pope appeared, a shout of recognition arose from the throng gathered in St. Peter's Square.

9. Study the words underlined. Look them up in your dictionary. Write the definitions in the space provided.

   People who live in remote areas of the world tend to preserve their language and culture.
   _*remote – distant; far*_____
   _*preserve – keep; retain*_____

10. Circle the letter of the sentence that corresponds to the meaning of the original sentence.

    The evidence in this report is unreliable because of the methods used.
    a. There is excellent evidence.
    b. There is no evidence.
    c. There is questionable evidence.

TEST FORMAT

The exercises below are the same exercises. But they are printed in test format.

1. Most people are <u>flattered</u> when we ask their opinions.

   a. happy because of praise
   b. frightened because of punishment
   c. angry because of criticism
   d. worried because of ignorance

2. What a very <u>amusing</u> story!

   a. strange
   b. serious
   c. funny
   d. true

3. Since the judge was _____, the man's lawyer was able to convince the jury of his client's innocence.

   a. sympathetic
   b. humorous
   c. disturbing
   d. dreadful

4. When you have a health problem, you should _____ a doctor.

   a. converse
   b. confuse
   c. confront
   d. consult

5. There seems to be a great deal of <u>physical force</u> on television.

   a. deceit
   b. violence
   c. greed
   d. envy

6. Some of the <u>signs of the disease</u> were difficult to understand, because they seemed to vary every day.

   a. signals
   b. symbols
   c. symptoms
   d. substitutes

7. One-celled forms of <u>water</u> animals may have been the first signs of life on this planet.

   a. avian
   b. canine
   c. human
   d. marine

8. When the Pope appeared, a shout of recognition arose from the <u>crowd</u> gathered in St. Peter's Square.

   a. herd
   b. throng
   c. flock
   d. swarm

9.   People who live in far-away areas of the world tend to preserve their language and culture.

    a.   remote
    b.   recent
    c.   distinct
    d.   expert

10.   The evidence in this report is unreliable because of the methods used.

    a.   excellent
    b.   questionable
    c.   encouraging
    d.   harmful

Can you recognize the information from your textbooks when it is printed in *test format*? If you can *learn to read for new vocabulary in context* in your textbooks and *recognize the information* when it is printed in test format, you are ready to take Part II of the Michigan Test of English Language Proficiency. You can apply your knowledge and skill to the test.

Answer Key

1.	a	6.	c
2.	c	7.	d
3.	a	8.	b
4.	d	9.	a
5.	b	10.	b

Part III—Reading Comprehension

On Part III of the Michigan Test of English Language Proficiency, you won't see exactly the same reading passages that you have studied in your textbooks. But you will see passages about the same kinds of topics—history, languages, literature, social science, physical science, and personal anecdotes. If you can read the passages in advanced-level reading textbooks, you should be able to read the passages on your test.

First, read the passages in your textbooks. Read every day. Use these passages to practice and improve your reading skills.

Now learn to apply the skills that you have practiced to the test. Practice the most important reading skills. Skim; scan; read longer phrases; read faster; read vocabulary in context without using a dictionary; and read for comprehension and inference.

OPTIONAL ASSIGNMENTS

Optional means something that you *may* or *may not* do. If you need more practice in structure, vocabulary, and reading comprehension, you may want to do some of the assignments suggested below. Ask your librarian or language lab assistant for the books you need.

Structure

1. Sharpe, Pamela J. *Barron's How to Prepare for the TOEFL (Test of English as a Foreign Language)*. Woodbury, New York: Barron's Educational Series, Inc., 1976.

    Study Chapter Three, "Review of Structure and Written Expression," and complete Section II, Part A of Model Tests 1-6. Use the Explanatory Answers in Chapter Six to check your answers. Section II, Part B is not assigned.

2. Sharpe, Pamela J. *Barron's Practice Exercises for the TOEFL (Test of English as a Foreign Language)*. Woodbury, New York: Barron's Educational Series, Inc., 1980.

    Complete Exercises 1-11 on pages 43-64.

Vocabulary

1. Bromberg, Murray, et al. *504 Absolutely Essential Words*. Woodbury, New York: Barron's Educational Series, Inc., 1975.

    Skim this book for new words.

2. Harris, David P. *Reading Improvement Exercises for Students of English as a Second Language*. Englewood Cliffs, New Jersey: Prentice-Hall, 1966.

    Complete the Diagnostic Vocabulary Test on pages 3-9. Study the words that you did not know the first time.

3. Thorndike, Edward Lee. *The Teacher's Word Book of 30,000 Words*. New York: Columbia University Press, 1944.

    Ask your librarian to show you how to use the *Teacher's Word Book*. This is the book that is used in selecting vocabulary words for Part II of the MTELP.
    Spend a few minutes looking for words in the 4,000-6,000 range. These are the words that are usually tested.
    Looking through this book should help you understand why it is so difficult to study vocabulary for the MTELP.
    You should not study the Teacher's Word Book. You should not even try to study the words in the 4,000-6,000 word range.
    What you should do is spend your time reading. The words in the 4,000-6,000 word range frequently appear in adult-level reading. In this way you will be studying vocabulary and improving your reading skills at the same time.

Reading Comprehension

1. Harris, David P. *Reading Improvement Exercises for Students of English as a Second Language*. Englewood Cliffs, New Jersey: Prentice-Hall, 1966.

   Read Parts Five-Eight on pages 55-155. Answer the comprehension questions. Parts Two-Four and Part Nine are not assigned.

2. Turner, David R. *Scoring High on Reading Tests*. New York: Arco, 1978.

   Read the book carefully, and answer all of the comprehension questions.
   There are a few readings included on poetry and drama on pages 125, 128, 129, 131, 132, 135, 163-179. They are not assigned.

3. Sharpe, Pamela J. *Barron's How to Prepare for the TOEFL (Test of English as a Foreign Language)*. Woodbury, New York: Barron's Educational Series, Inc., 1976.

   Complete section III, Part B of Model Tests 1-6. Use the Explanatory Answers in Chapter Six to check your answers. Section III, Part A is not assigned.

4. Sharpe, Pamela J. *Barron's Practice Exercises for the TOEFL (Test of English as a Foreign Language)*. Woodbury, New York: Barron's Educational Series, Inc., 1980.

   Complete Exercises Six-Thirteen on pages 102-142.

5. Baudoin, Margaret E. et al. *Reader's Choice*. Ann Arbor, Michigan: University of Michigan Press, 1977.

   Complete Paragraph Reading on pages 20-25, 51-54, 82-85; Paragraph Analysis on pages 117-127; Paragraph Reading on pages 157-159.

6. Hirasawa, Louise, and Markstein, Linda. *Developing Reading Skills*. Rowley, Massachusetts: Newbury House, 1974.

   Complete the timed Readings 1-12, and Part A after each reading.

7. Markstein, Linda, and Hirasawa, Louise. *Expanding Reading Skills*. Rowley, Massachusetts: Newbury House, 1977.

   Complete the Timed Readings 1-12, and Part A after each reading.

8. Sack, Allan, and Yourman, Jack. *88 Passages to Develop Reading Comprehension*. New York: College Skills Center, 1968.

   Read the book carefully, and answer all of the Comprehension Questions.

9. Sack, Allan, and Yourman, Jack. *100 Passages to Develop Reading Comprehension*. New York: College Skills Center, 1965.

   Read the book carefully, and answer all of the Comprehension Questions.

10. Farley, Eugene, and Farley, Alice. *Barron's Developing Reading Skills for the High School Equivalency Examinations*. Woodbury, New York: Barron's Educational Series, Inc., 1972.

Complete the following lessons:

Lesson 5	Finding The Main Idea, Pages 35-44
Lesson 6	Finding Facts, Pages 44-55
Review Section A	Pages 69-76
Lesson 8	Reading To Study And Learn, Pages 77-86
Lesson 9	Understanding Inferences, Pages 87-97
Lesson 10	More on Inferences, Pages 98-110
Lesson 18	Reading Interpretation In Natural Sciences, Pages 244-256
Lesson 22	Reading Interpretation in Literature, Pages 325-337
Practice Passages	Pages 356-360

11. Rockowitz, Murray. *Barron's How to Prepare for the High School Equivalency Examination (GED)*. Woodbury, New York: Barron's Educational Series, Inc., 1979.

Complete the following selections:

Selections 6-19	Pages 278-292
Selections 1-21	Pages 382-403
Selections 1-13	Pages 442-453
Selections 1-8	Pages 492-500
Selections 1-6	Pages 508-513
Selections 1-10	Pages 734-744
Selections 1-10	Pages 747-756
Selections 1-10	Pages 761-770
Selections 1-10	Pages 811-821
Selections 1-7	Pages 825-830

Complete Test 4, The Reading Skills Test, Pages 838-848

Practicing Composition

The Michigan
Composition Test

CHAPTER 6

The Michigan Composition Test

DESCRIPTION OF THE TEST

The Michigan Composition Test is a test of your ability to write a short composition, one or one and a half pages in length. There are usually three topics from which to choose. It is very important that you understand the topics, because your paper will not be graded if you write about a topic other than one of the assigned topics. If you do not understand the topics, you should ask the examiner to explain them to you or translate them for you.

The topics often include: Opinions, Personal Experiences, Descriptions, Comparisons, and Imagined Situations.

Compositions are graded for organization and correctness of expression. The grader must be able to understand what you mean. Either formal or informal style is acceptable. Compositions are *not* graded for ideas, opinions, the accuracy of information such as names and dates, or the appearance of the handwriting. They are not read for capitalization, punctuation, or spelling.

Don't spend time writing a perfect outline. Your outline will *not* be graded.

Don't recopy your composition. It is a waste of time. Your paper will *not* be graded for neatness. Use the time to re-read and correct your paper instead.

Since you may not use dictionaries or other books to help you in writing the composition, you will probably make some spelling errors. Try to spell words correctly, but if you are not sure of a word, spell it the way it sounds.

The test is timed. The examiner will collect the papers at the end of thirty minutes.

Sample Topics

Opinion: In some states, it is possible for a married couple to get a divorce simply because they no longer want to be married. What is your opinion of this kind of law?

Personal Experience: Do you consider yourself a realist or an idealist? Relate a personal experience that illustrates this characteristic.

Description: Describe the person who has helped you most in your life.

Comparison: In the United States, it is customary for girls and boys to attend the same schools. Is this educational system the same as or different from that of your country? How is it the same? How is it different?

Imagined Situation: Imagine that you had been born in the United States. How would your life have been different?

COMPOSITION MODEL TEST ONE

1 Question

30 Minutes

Directions

In this test, you will have thirty minutes to write a composition. There are three topics to choose from. You must choose *one* of the assigned topics and write about it, or your paper will not be graded.

Some examiners will read the topics; other examiners will write the topics.

Choose only *one* of the topics for your composition. Write one to one and a half pages.

You must stop writing at the end of thirty minutes.

---

1. If you could change one day in your life, which day would you change? How would your life be different now?

2. In the United States, it is considered bad luck to walk under a ladder. Black cats and the number thirteen are also considered unlucky. What are some things that are considered bad luck in your country?

3. What is your opinion of welfare? (Welfare is a system under which the government helps provide food, housing, and services like health care for people who cannot afford to pay for them.) Explain your reasons.

COMPOSITION MODEL TEST TWO

1 Question

30 Minutes

Directions

In this test, you will have thirty minutes to write a composition. There are three topics to choose from. You must choose *one* of the assigned topics and write about it, or your paper will not be graded.

Some examiners will read the topics; other examiners will write the topics.

Choose only *one* of the topics for your composition. Write one to one and a half pages.

You must stop writing at the end of thirty minutes.

---

1. Your friend wants to borrow your car. You know that he does not have a driver's license. You also know that he will be angry if you refuse. What do you say? What do you do? Explain your reasons.

2. Should older people live with their adult children? Explain why you think this is a good or a bad practice.

3. Who is the person that you respect most? Why?

COMPOSITION MODEL TEST THREE

1 Question

30 Minutes

Directions

In this test, you will have thirty minutes to write a composition. There are three topics to choose from. You must choose *one* of the assigned topics and write about it, or your paper will not be graded.

Some examiners will read the topics; other examiners will write the topics.

Choose only *one* of the topics for your composition. Write one to one and a half pages.

You must stop writing at the end of thirty minutes.

---

1. In some states, a person who is convicted of possession of marijuana can spend many years in jail. Do you agree or disagree with this punishment? Why?

2. Is it better to encourage individuality or conformity in the members of a society? Which trait would you want your children to have?

3. "The best-laid plans of mice and men often go astray." Relate a personal experience that illustrates this saying.

Grader's Checklist

You will need to ask your teacher or a friend who speaks English to help you grade your composition tests. Give this Grader's Checklist to your helper to use when reviewing your composition.

Organization

First, read the composition for organization.

✓ **Is there a *topic sentence* or *thesis statement*?**
The topic sentence is an introduction to the composition. It states the main idea. In a composition for the Michigan Composition Test, it is often a restatement of the question.

✓ **Are there *support statements* or *examples*?**
Support statements contain information or examples to convince the reader that the main idea is correct.

✓ **Are the *transition words* used correctly?**
Transition words are used to join sentences and to join paragraphs. Examples of transition words:

order: first, second, next, then, last

addition: furthermore, in addition

example: for example, for instance

contrast: in contrast, on the other hand

concession: although, since, because

consequence: therefore, consequently

conclusion: in conclusion, in summary

✓ **Does the composition have *unity*?**
Unity means that every sentence is about the same topic. Other topics, unrelated to the main idea, are not included.

✓ **Does the composition have *coherence*?**
Coherence means that the sentences seem to be in the correct order. It is easy to understand what is being said.

Correctness

Now read the composition again. This time, use a pencil to mark for correctness. Draw a circle around each error and give the writer an opportunity to correct it. If he or she does not recognize the error, then you should correct it and explain it if possible.

✔ **Are all of the sentences *complete?***
Check for stated or implied subjects and verbs in each sentence.

✔ **Are the *verb forms* correct?**
Check for -*s*, -*ed*, and -*ing* endings. Check for auxiliaries such as *am, is, are, was, were, do, does, did, have, has, had*. Non-native speakers of English often forget to include them with main verbs.

✔ **Is there *agreement* between subject and verb? Between noun or pronoun and antecedent?**
Check for singular verbs with singular subjects, and plural verbs with plural subjects. Check for singular nouns or pronouns with singular antecedents, and plural nouns or pronouns with plural antecedents.

✔ **Are *function words* used correctly?**
Check for correct use of prepositions, conjunctions, and adverbs. Circle any function words that are used in a confusing or illogical way.

✔ **Is *parallel structure* used correctly?**
Check for the same grammatical structures in a list or series, and after correlatives like *both . . . and, not . . . but, either . . . or,* and *neither . . . nor*.

NOTE: Do *not* read this composition for errors in capitalization, punctuation, and spelling.

Sample Composition

A marked composition is printed below as an example.

Question: The Civil Aeronautics Board and the Federal Aviation Administration are considering whether to ban cigarette smoking on airplanes. In your opinion, should people be allowed to smoke on airplanes? Why or why not?

In my opinion, people should not be allowed to smoke on airplanes. They should not be allowed to smoke for three reasons.

GOOD THESIS STATEMENT.

First, smoking is not enjoyed by everyone on the airplane. Nevertheless, even when certain seats are reserved for non-smokers, the smell of smoke cannot be restricted to the smoking area.

GOOD USE OF TRANSITIONS FIRST SECOND LAST THEREFORE.

Second, smoking is a dirty practice. If the airlines did not have to pay for personnel to clean ashes and cigarette butts from ashtrays, floors, and seats, and if they did not have to replace floor coverings and seat covers because of cigarette burns, perhaps air travel would be a little less expensive.

Last, there is always danger of fire aboard an airplane, especially in the event of a crash. Smoking increases that danger.

GOOD SUPPORT STATEMENTS.

Therefore, I recommend that the Civil Aeronautics Board and the Federal Aviation Administration ban cigarette smoking on airplanes.

GOOD CONCLUDING STATEMENT

Continued Study
For Composition

CHAPTER 7

Continued Study For Composition

A THREE-STEP STUDY PROGRAM

Because the Michigan Composition Test requires that you write an original composition, you must develop both your knowledge of English composition and your skill in writing.

You can do this by following three steps:

1. **Study one or more advanced-level composition textbooks** to review your knowledge of the skills needed in planning, writing, and editing compositions.

2. **Practice writing compositions** with topics like those used on the Michigan Composition Test to improve your skill in writing.

3. **Apply your knowledge and skill to the test.**

Step One: Study One or More Good Advanced-Level Composition Textbooks

There are many good composition books. Those of you who are enrolled in an English program probably have a good composition book. *Attend your composition class every day*. The best preparation for the Michigan Composition Test is daily practice in writing and correcting compositions.

If you are not enrolled in an English program, buy a good advanced-level composition book or borrow one from the library. There are dozens of good books. Some of them are listed below:

Bander, Robert G. *American English Rhetoric*. New York: Holt, Rinehart and Winston, Inc., 1971.

Bander, Robert G. *From Sentence to Paragraph. A Writing Workbook in English as a Second Language*. New York: Holt, Rinehart and Winston, Inc, 1980.

Lawrence, Mary S. *Reading, Thinking, Writing: A Text for Students of English as a Second Language*. Ann Arbor, Michigan: University of Michigan Press, 1975.

Lawrence, Mary S. *Writing as a Thinking Process*. Ann Arbor, Michigan: University of Michigan Press, 1976.

McKay, Sandra, and Rosenthal, Lisa. *Writing for a Specific Purpose*. Englewood Cliffs, New Jersey: Prentice-Hall, 1980.

Seale, Barbara. *Writing Efficiently: A Step by Step Composition Course*. Englewood Cliffs, New Jersey: Prentice-Hall, 1978.

Sullivan, Kathleen E. *Paragraph Practice*. New York: Macmillan Co., Inc., 1976.

Step Two: Practice Writing Compositions with Topics Like Those Used on the Michigan Composition Test

There are five kinds of specific topics that you should practice. They are listed below, with examples from the model tests in this book.

Specific Topics

1. OPINION

Example

In some states, a person who is arrested for possession of marijuana can spend many years in jail. Do you agree or disagree with this punishment? Why?

2. PERSONAL EXPERIENCE

Example

"The best laid plans of mice and men often go astray." Relate a personal experience that illustrates this saying.

3. DESCRIPTION

Example

Who is the person that you respect most? Why?

4. COMPARISON

Example

In the United States it is considered bad luck to walk under a ladder. Black cats and the number thirteen are also considered unlucky. What are some things that are considered bad luck in your country?

5. IMAGINED SITUATION

Example

Your friend wants to borrow your car. You know that he does not have a driver's license. You also know that he will be angry if you refuse. What do you say? What do you do?

Step Three: Apply Your Knowledge and Skill to the Test

To apply your knowledge and skill means to use information that you have already studied to help you in a new situation.

On the Michigan Composition Test, you won't see exactly the same composition questions that you have studied in your textbooks. But you will see questions about the same kind of topics—opinions, personal experiences, descriptions, comparisons, and imagined situations. If you can write compositions about the topics in advanced-level composition textbooks, you should be able to write a composition about one of the topics on your test.

First, write compositions about the topics in your textbooks. Write every day. Use this practice to improve your writing skills.

Now learn to apply the skills that you have practiced to the test. Write a topic sentence or thesis statement, support statements or examples, and a concluding statement. Check your composition for structure, agreement, parallelism, correct transitions, unity, and coherence. Remember, a good writer must also learn to correct his or her composition after it is written.

OPTIONAL ASSIGNMENTS

Optional means something that you *may* or *may not* do. If you need more practice in writing compositions, you may want to do some of the assignments suggested below. Ask your librarian or language lab assistant for the books you need.

1. Bander, Robert G. *From Sentence to Paragraph: A Writing Workbook in English as a Second Language*. New York: Holt, Rinehart and Winston, 1980.

    Complete all of the exercises in the workbook.

2. Lawrence, Mary S. *Writing as a Thinking Process*. Ann Arbor, Michigan: University of Michigan, 1976.

Complete the following exercises and show them to your English teacher or an American friend.

Introducing Generalizations and Specifics	Pages 63-70
Introducing Comparison and Contrast	Pages 81-96
Introducing Hypothesis	Pages 178-183
Introducing Proposals	Pages 184-189
Introducing Personal Opinion	Pages 190-196
Introducing Refutation	Pages 197-199
Introducing Discussion	Pages 200-204

3. Sullivan, Kathleen E. *Paragraph Practice*. New York: Macmillan Publishing Co., Inc., 1967.

Complete the following exercises and show them to your English teacher or an American friend.

Describe someone's face
Exercise 3   Page 41

Describe your favorite forms of weekend entertainment
Exercise 4   Page 42

Describe an interesting incident
Exercise 5   Page 43

Discuss the sort of wife you want to be (have)
Exercise 7   Pages 45

Discuss a principle or lesson you would teach a child
Exercise 8   Page 46

Discuss your favorite class
Exercise 9   Page 47

Discuss a hobby or pastime
Exercise 10   Page 48

Discuss a character in a story
Exercise 2   Page 54

Write about your biggest problem in college
Exercise 3   Page 56

Make a comparison by showing similarities
Exercise 7   Page 68

Make a comparison (contrast) by showing differences
Exercise 8   Page 69

Propose a change in the existing state of affairs
Exercise 9   Page 72

Give one reason in support of your proposed change
Exercise 10   Page 75

Describe an unpleasant sensory experience
Exercise 1   Page 79

Describe a pleasant sensory experience
Exercise 2   Page 80

Describe an experience in flashback form
Exercise 3   Page 81

Describe a moment when you found or learned something new
Exercise 4   Page 82

Discuss a quotation
Exercise 6   Page 84

Write what would happen if . . .
Exercise 7   Page 85

Describe someone you see often
Exercise 8   Page 86

Also study the notes on ages 89-94, and Chapter IX "Practicing the Thesis Sentence" on pages 108-113.

4. McKay, Sandra, and Rosenthal, Lisa. *Writing for a Specific Purpose*. Englewood Cliffs, New Jersey: Prentice-Hall, 1980.

Complete the exercises in the following chapters and show them to your English teacher or an American friend.

Chapter 7	"Recommend"	Pages 99-109
Chapter 8	"Agree/Disagree"	Pages 110-123

5. Seale, Barbara. *Writing Efficiently*. Englewood Cliffs, New Jersey: Prentice-Hall, 1978.

Study the following chapters and discuss them with your English teacher or an American friend.

Chapter III	"Argumentative Themes"	Pages 76-147
Chapter IV	"Judging and Polishing Paragraphs and Themes"	Pages 149-187

6. Traiger, Arthur, and Gersten, Leon. *Solutions to Your Writing Problems*. Woodbury, New York: Barron's Educational Series, Inc., 1980.

Study Chapter Three, Pages 79-100

7. Bromberg, Murray, and Liebb, Julius. *You Can Succeed in Reading and Writing*. Woodbury, New York: Barron's Educational Series, Inc., 1981.

Review Steps 12, 15, 16, 17, 18, 20, and 25 on Pages 69, 87, 93, 99, 105, 117, and 151.

Transcript for the Model Tests of Aural Comprehension

APPENDIX

Transcript for the Model Tests of Aural Comprehension

TRANSCRIPT—AURAL COMPREHENSION TESTS

The following is a transcript for Model Tests of Aural Comprehension One, Two, and Three.

When you take the model tests in this book, you should use the available cassette. You will find Model Tests of Aural Comprehension One, Two, and Three on the cassette.

If you have someone read the model test transcript to you instead, be sure that he or she uses the correct timing. The reader should use a stop watch, or a regular watch with a second hand. *There should be a twelve-second pause after each question or statement.*

Be sure that the reader speaks clearly and at a moderate pace. Answer choices and answer sheets for each of the three tests may be found in chaper 2.

MODEL TEST ONE

Directions

This is a test of your ability to understand spoken English structure. There are ninety problems in this test, with three possible answers for each problem. You will hear either a question or a statement. When you hear a question, read the three possible answers, (a), (b), and (c). Choose the one that would be the best answer to the question. When you hear a statement, read the three possible answers, (a), (b), and (c). Choose the one that would be closest in meaning to the statement you have heard.

Look at the sample test items on page 26. When you have reviewed them, the test will begin. Refer to the answer choices on pages 27-30 as the transcript is read to you. Remember, you will hear the statement or question only once, and you have 12 seconds to select and mark your answers.

---

1. Are the tests graded yet?

2. Are you sure that the secretary sent a copy of the I-20?

3. I'd planned to see the movie, but I also read the book.

4. It usually snows in February.

5. The buses don't stop running until eight o'clock.

6. I told John to write the paper for me.

7. I decided to study at City College, because State University had already closed admissions and Community College didn't accept my transfer credit.

8. I've never heard the orchestra play more professionally.

9. Is Bob very busy?

10. Shall I buy some oranges?

11. Mabel was surprised when Tom and I were arrested by the police.

12. How many students are from Saudi Arabia?

13. Has the official letter been sent to the embassy already?

14. Is Ruth taking her vacation next week?

15. Tom called her before we received her letter.

16. Isn't their phone number in the book?

17. Joe wasn't very hungry.

18. Are the Williamses here yet?

19. This letter is his, and so is the package over there.

20. Bill and Betty didn't leave until classes were over on Friday.

21. Did you finish the course or drop it?

22. When we went to Betty's house, her father was well, wasn't he?

23. Will you have some tea?

24. Is that woman the best tutor?

25. I'll always remember my first day here when the man from the university met me at the airport.

26. Is it correct that you're employed as a secretary on campus?

27. Ruth told her doctor when the baby was due.

28. Did you feel confident about passing the course?

29. This game is supposed to be very good, but I will not be able to go see it.

30. Wasn't the woman's husband there when she arrived at the airport?

31. Our neighbors have been friendlier.

32. Anna's certificate will be given to her husband at the ceremony on Friday.

33. The students and the foreign student advisor were helped.

34. Where was your secretary?

35. She'd just finished cutting the cake when I arrived.

36. Did Philip and Jane tell you for certain that they were getting a divorce?

37. Everybody knows where the office is, but who's the director?

38. Whatever happened, Linda wasn't going to go home winter quarter.

39. Do you know if the Browns are still living in Tucson?

40. I can't remember the family who visited you.

41. Has she accepted Pete's proposal?

42. Does it take a long time to travel from your country to the United States?

43. Was there any problem?

44. James wondered who would win.

45. What kind of sports events are the most popular in your country?

46. It didn't start raining until the afternoon of the wedding.

47. They asked me where the car was parked.

48. Where did Mr. Wilson send his son to school?

49. The climate is very good, but we'll probably not go there to live.

50. James wasn't angry, even though it was our fault.

51. Who works at the library?

52. How is John's arm now?

53. I know what the address is, but how do you get there?

54. Which of these two typewriters do you think I should buy?

55. Couldn't you have changed your plane reservation if you had wanted to?

56. Mrs. Jones has finished typing your report, hasn't she?

57. The University of Southern California and UCLA were both beaten in the last game of the season.

58. Do you have any homework tonight?

59. They had no problems that I am aware of.

60. Could Philip finish his homework if he tried?

61. We have no teacher who's not from the United States.

62. Do you like to drink?

63. Bill won't tell her, and I won't either.

64. Who did you sell your furniture to?

65. Did Al know that you borrowed his car?

66. John has never been sick.

67. Bill is going to graduate this quarter, but his cousin isn't.

68. Do the girls that you live with in the dorm help you with your English?

69. Do people from your country usually like the food here?

70. What will Mr. Johnson ever do with these?

71. Miss Smith doesn't stop practicing at five o'clock.

72. How many times did you take the class?

73. There are no seats left for the movie that we wanted to see.

74. We're invited, but we aren't able to go.

75. What did Betty's brother give her for her birthday?

76. I took an efficiency, because the one-bedroom wasn't furnished and the two-bedroom was too expensive.

77. Mary told the taxi driver that he should wait for me.

78. The workbook wasn't used at all.

79. I asked for a glass of water and a cup of coffee, but the waitress didn't give me the water.

80. I bought the red coat, because the black one was too big and the brown one wasn't heavy enough.

81. Who's calling, please?

82. He stopped smoking because his wife asked him to.

83. We were going to stop in London on the way home, but we stopped in Paris instead.

84. I forgot the name of the teacher whom you recommended.

85. I understand that you're going to transfer, but when are you leaving?

86. They have a child who doesn't go to nursery school.

87. I was upset because John didn't help his sister find an apartment.

88. John continued working in spite of what his doctor said.

89. Mary told me she would study with my roommate.

90. How much does it cost to take the Michigan Test?

MODEL TEST TWO

Directions

This is a test of your ability to understand spoken English structure. There are ninety problems in this test, with three possible answers for each problem. You will hear either a question or a statement. When you hear a question, read the three possible answers, (a), (b), and (c). Choose the one that would be the best answer to the question. When you hear a statement, read the three possible answers, (a), (b), and (c). Choose the one that would be closest in meaning to the statement you have heard.

Look at the sample test items on page 26. When you have reviewed them, the test will begin. Refer to the answer choices on pages 27-30 as the transcript is read to you. Remember, you will hear the statement or question only once, and you have 12 seconds to select and mark your answers.

1. Have the tests been graded yet?

2. Is this a copy of the I-20 that the secretary sent?

3. I'd planned to read the book, but I saw the movie instead.

4. It doesn't snow at all in February.

5. The buses don't start running until eight o'clock.

6. Alice told me to write the paper for John.

7. I decided to study at State University, because City College didn't offer my major and Community College didn't accept my transfer credit.

8. I've heard the orchestra play more professionally.

9. Is the line busy?

10. Do you have any fresh fish today?

11. Tom and I were surprised when Mabel was arrested by the police.

12. How much is the tuition for this class?

13. Did the officials send the letter to the embassy yet?

14. Is next week when Ruth is taking her vacation?

15. Tom called her in spite of our receiving her letter.

16. Isn't Mabel going to get a phone?

17. Joe was really hungry.

18. Is William here yet?

19. This letter isn't his, and the package isn't either.

20. Bill and Betty left before classes had started on Friday.

21. You were sorry that you had to drop the course, weren't you?

22. Was Betty at home when you went to see her father?

23. Does that tea have enough sugar in it?

24. What kind of person is a good tutor?

25. I'll always remember the man from the university who met me at the airport my first day here.

26. Is the secretary correct that you're employed on campus?

27. Ruth asked the doctor when the baby was due.

28. Did you pass the course or fail it?

29. This game is supposed to be very good, and I'm going to see it.

30. Wasn't the woman's daughter there when she arrived at the airport?

31. Our neighbors have never been friendly.

32. Jim's certificate will be given to his wife at the ceremony on Friday.

33. The students were helped by the foreign student advisor.

34. Where did your secretary go?

35. I arrived just as she was cutting the cake.

36. Is Philip certain that Jane is getting a divorce?

37. Everybody knows who the director is, but where's his office?

38. Linda wasn't going to go home until winter quarter.

39. Do you know if Mrs. Brown is still living in Tucson?

40. I can't remember the family whom you visited.

41. Would she have accepted if Pete had proposed?

42. Do you plan to take your family on a trip when they come to visit you?

43. Were there any problems?

44. James told me who would win.

45. Which sports event is the most popular in your country?

46. It didn't start raining on the afternoon of the wedding.

47. We wondered where we had parked the car.

48. What kind of school does Mr. Wilson want his son to attend?

49. The climate is good, and we have to go there to live.

50. Whatever James may think, it wasn't our fault.

51. Who's going to meet you at the library?

52. Which arm did John break?

53. I know generally how to get there, but what's the address?

54. What does a good typewriter cost in the United States?

55. Couldn't you change your plane reservation if you wanted to?

56. The report is finished, isn't it?

57. The University of Southern California was beaten by UCLA in the last football game of the season.

58. Do you have any exams this week?

59. They had a few problems that I am aware of.

60. Has Philip finished doing his homework?

61. We have no teacher who's from the United States.

62. Would you like some more tea?

63. Bill won't tell her, but I will.

64. Who sold your furniture for you?

65. Did you borrow Al's car without telling him?

66. John has never been sicker.

67. Bill is going to graduate this quarter, and so is his cousin.

68. Does it help you learn English to live in the dorm?

69. Does the food in your country have rice in it?

70. Will Mr. Johnson ever give this his consideration?

71. Miss Smith doesn't stop practicing until five o'clock.

72. How many students registered for the class?

73. There are seats left for the movie that we want to see.

74. We're invited, and we have to go.

75. Where was Betty when her brother called her last night?

76. I took a one-bedroom because the efficiency was too small and the two-bedroom was too expensive.

77. I told Mary that she should wait for the taxi driver.

78. The workbook wasn't all used.

79. I asked for a cup of coffee, but the waitress gave me a glass of water instead.

80. I bought the black coat because the red one was too expensive and the brown one wasn't warm enough.

81. Who do you want to charge the call to?

82. He stopped smoking even though his wife hadn't asked him to.

83. We were only going to stop in London on the way home, but we stopped in Paris, too.

84. I forgot the name of the course that the teacher recommended.

85. I understand that you're going to transfer, but where are you going?

86. They have no children who don't go to nursery school.

87. I was upset because John and his sister didn't help me find an apartment.

88. John continued working because his doctor had said he could.

89. My roommate told Mary he'd study with me.

90. How many times did you take the Michigan Test before you scored 80?

MODEL TEST THREE

Directions

This is a test of your ability to understand spoken English structure. There are ninety problems in this test, with three possible answers for each problem. You will hear either a question or a statement. When you hear a question, read the three possible answers, (a), (b), and (c). Choose the one that would be the best answer to the question. When you hear a statement, read the three possible answers, (a), (b), and (c). Choose the one that would be closest in meaning to the statement you have heard.

Look at the sample test items on page 26. When you have reviewed them, the test will begin. Refer to the answer choices on pages 27-30 as the transcript is read to you. Remember, you will hear the statement or question only once, and you have 12 seconds to select and mark your answers.

---

1. Will the tests be returned today?

2. Is the secretary sure that she sent a copy of the I-20?

3. I'd planned to see the movie, but I read the book instead.

4. It doesn't snow very often in February.

5. The buses don't start running at eight o'clock.

6. John told Alice to write the paper for me.

7. I decided to study at Community College, because State University had already closed admissions and City College didn't offer my major.

8. I've never heard the orchestra play professionally.

9. Is Mary very busy?

10. Shall I buy some milk?

11. Mabel and I were surprised when Tom was arrested by the police.

12. How many times have students from Saudi Arabia enrolled in your class?

13. Have the officials been sent to the embassy already?

14. Is it next week or the week after that Ruth is taking her vacation?

15. Tom called her because we'd received her letter.

16. Isn't James going to get a phone?

17. Joe wasn't hungry at all.

18. Is William's check here yet?

19. This letter is his, but the package isn't.

20. Bill and Betty left for vacation before classes were over on Friday.

21. Did you finally decide what to do about your courses?

22. I know that her father is well now, but where's he staying?

23. Is that tea strong enough?

24. Which person is the best tutor?

25. The man from the university whom I met at the airport my first day here will never forget me.

26. Were you employed as a secretary on campus?

27. Ruth wondered if the doctor was due.

28. Did failing the course mean you had to repeat it?

29. This game isn't supposed to be very good, but I'll probably go see it.

30. Wasn't the woman's suitcase with her when she arrived at the airport?

31. Our neighbors have never been friendlier.

32. Jim and his wife are going to be given their certificates at the ceremony on Friday.

33. The foreign student advisor was helped by the students.

34. What's your secretary's responsibility?

35. She hadn't begun to cut the cake when I arrived.

36. Is it certain that Philip and Jane are getting a divorce?

37. All of the students know the director, don't they?

38. Linda was going to go home until winter quarter.

39. Do you know if Tucson is still a good place to live?

40. I can't remember the family whose house you visited.

41. Would she accept if Pete proposed?

42. Does your family like to travel a lot?

43. Was it any problem?

44. James asked me who would win.

45. When are sports events popular in your country?

46. It didn't stop raining until the afternoon of the wedding.

47. They told me where the car was parked.

48. From which school did Mr. Wilson's son get his degree?

49. The climate is not very good, but we ought to go there to live.

50. Was James angry because we couldn't decide whose fault it was?

51. Who are you taking the book out for?

52. How did John break his arm?

53. I know your address, but what's your telephone number?

54. What kind of typewriter costs the most?

55. Haven't you changed your plane reservation yet?

56. The report has been finished, hasn't it?

57. UCLA was beaten by the University of Southern California in the last game of the season.

58. Do you want any coffee while you're studying?

59. They had a few problems that I wasn't aware of.

60. Could Philip have finished his homework if he'd tried?

61. We have a teacher who's not from the United States.

62. Would you like some more cookies?

63. I'll tell her, and so will Bill.

64. Who's selling your furniture?

65. Did Al's car start okay when you borrowed it?

66. John has been sicker.

67. Bill isn't going to graduate this quarter, and his cousin isn't either.

68. Do you live in the dorm so that you can learn English with the girls?

69. Is the food in your country like the food here?

70. Whatever Mr. Johnson does, it's all right with me.

71. Miss Smith doesn't start practicing until five o'clock.

72. How much does the book cost for that class?

73. I know that these seats are right.

74. We weren't invited, but we went.

75. Where did Betty's brother take her last night?

76. I took a two-bedroom because the one-bedroom was unfurnished and the efficiency was too small.

77. Mary told me that I should wait for the taxi driver.

78. All of the workbook was used.

79. I asked for a cup of coffee, but the waitress gave me some water, too.

80. I bought the brown coat, because the red one was too expensive and the black one was too big.

81. Who uses this credit card to make calls?

82. His wife kept smoking in spite of him.

83. We were going to stop in London and Paris on the way home, but we didn't stop in Paris.

84. I forgot the name of the teacher who recommended you.

85. I understand that you're going to transfer, but why are you doing it?

86. They have no children who go to nursery school.

87. I was upset because John's sister didn't help him find an apartment.

88. John stopped working even though his doctor had said that he could continue.

89. Mary told my roommate she'd study with me.

90. How many of your friends took the Michigan Test with you?

HOW TO PREPARE FOR THE
MICHIGAN TEST BATTERY

LISTENING CASSETTE

For the Michigan Battery Aural Comprehension Test in This Book

STUDENTS' #1 CHOICE

BARRON'S
HOW TO PREPARE FOR THE
MICHIGAN TEST BATTERY

Pamela J. Sharpe

A complete guide to one of the most widely used tests of English for speakers of other languages— Required for admission and placement by hundreds of U.S. colleges and universities.

Covers all 3 tests in the Michigan Test Battery: Aural Comprehension • English Proficiency • Composition

Important Note: Even if you are taking the TOEFL (Test of English as a Foreign Language), you may still be required to take the Michigan Test Battery before beginning college work in the United States.

Includes: Tips on how to apply for, prepare for, and score high on the Michigan Tests Expert guidance to help you focus on the topics most likely to give you trouble 3 complete model test batteries with answers and explanations

LISTENING CASSETTE AVAILABLE (SEE DETAILS INSIDE)

The aural portion of the Michigan Test Battery measures your ability to understand spoken English. The only way you can practice for this part of the exam is to have the aural material read aloud to you. If you can't find anyone with a good command of English, or if you prefer to work on your own, you'll want to use the special Listening Cassette that Barron's has created especially for readers of this book.

The cassette, which can be used with any cassette tape player, covers all three aural comprehension tests in the book. You listen to the spoken questions on the recorder, and mark the correct answer choice in the book. The recording gives you time to make your responses, just as on the real exam.

ISBN 978-0-8120-2564-4

Please visit **www.barronseduc.com**
to view current prices and to order books

Barron's Educational Series, Inc.
250 Wireless Boulevard, Hauppauge, NY 11788

(#163) R 7/08